You're Stupid.

www.azrienoch.com

Smith-Luedke, Jeff

You're Stupid: How to Argue Effectively,
or The Neo-Machiavellian.
Includes bibliographical references.
ISBN-13: 978-0-557-38951-3

Cover art by Mike Fahl
www.mikefahl.com

You're stupid.

How to Argue Effectively

or

THE NEO-MACHAVELLIAN

By Jeff Smith-Luedke

Lulu, Inc.

Morrisville, NC

For Chaim Perelman,

who led a self-styled cripple to walk.

Table of contents

Winning 31

Strawman 224

Logic 233

Dishonesty 53

Contrastruction 214

Identity 240

Introduction 1

Insults 252

Index 266

You're stupid.

Language 6

Rhetoric 13   Instruction 17

Vocabulary 38

Contradiction 108

Obfuscation 171

The Means 205

Might 210

Authority 118

The Rules 49

Surreality 144

Extremes 131

Derailment 154

THE NE●-MACHIAVELLIAN 180

Presentation 87

Boredom 74

Laughter 80

Minimalism 100

Audiences 65

Everything in this book is a lie.

Now that all the people are gone who were looking for an excuse to put this book down, or who were looking for what they needed to discredit the book, we are left with only the people that want to learn to argue effectively. This will not be difficult. Everything in this book you already know, whether you're aware of it or not. And you already use it, whether you agree with it or not.

This book is not subtitled, "How to Argue Logically," or "How to Argue Fairly," but "How to Argue Effectively." That's what rhetoric is all about—achieving your goals using language. The tactics in this book apply to everything, from everyday conversations to formal debate forums to those irritating phone calls with debt collectors. It is meant to be read from beginning to end, and I recommend this approach for you this first time around. After that, do what you will. Skipping around, flaunting your attention deficiency, will leave you with a poorer understanding of what you have read than you would have otherwise. I do not want this book to be tedious or inaccessible to newcomers to philosophy, so I avoided philosophy for its own sake as best I could except where necessary, such as the discussion on language and Truth, as I believe the notion of Truth we were all brought up to respect is the greatest obstacle to effective argumentation. After the discussion on Truth, we will explore the broader structures of arguments, and finally we will explore the finer details of arguments.

This book's second title is, <u>The Neo-Machiavellian</u>. *Machiavellian*, according to some dictionary you probably don't care to know (in case you do, it's the Oxford English Dictionary), means, "The employment of cunning and duplicity in statecraft or in general conduct." Cunning and duplicitous politicking, broadened to the whole of argumentation, is also what this book is about. I do not encourage you to lower your moral standards, but I do encourage you to embrace the sneaky methods you already use to persuade people, even if you don't know you use them. Broadening *Machiavellian* to the whole of rhetoric is where we get the *neo-* in *neo-Machiavellian*. All the papers I've seen on neo-Machiavellian movements are about politics, specifically. That's not neo-Machiavellianism. That's Machiavellianism. You must misapply something to the point of complete irrelevance to have a real neo-movement. And I think I've done that well here.

Lastly, this book's proper title is, <u>You're Stupid</u>.

This isn't because you're stupid. You're not. But I'm saying it anyway.

Except where I have quoted someone, I have not cited sources. I do not know how to cite an inspiration in the midst of inspiration. So before I get inspired, I am indebted to the work of Chaim Perelman, Ludwig Wittgenstein, Jacques Derrida, Friedrich Nietzsche, Albert Camus, and Niccolò Machiavelli, more or less in that order as it pertains to rhetoric. The work of these men has influenced me a great deal, and I adore them for it. But, while this book is rhetorical, it is not argumentative, so calling upon authorities of the subject by paraphrasing their work simply isn't necessary. Even in the short discussion on language and Truth, I will state the perspective you need to have in order to make the most of the instructions. I will do this until I feel it is sufficiently explained, and not always until I feel the position is undeniable. Any argument for these positions you feel is necessary, you will find in my previous book, <u>The Absurdity of Philosophy</u>.

I would like to thank everyone who has supported my work in any of its forms, especially those who have challenged me. In particular, Mike Fahl, the artist who designed the cover, my wife, Andrea, and my dear friend, Karen. It's because of you that my sword is sharp. And my editor, April Jacobs. Without you, people would know me for the bumbling idiot I am.

All language is instructional and rhetorical. It is instructional because every phrase uttered, every word said, every description, question, abstraction, summary, etc., isn't just information about the person speaking, but information *to be used.* There is an important difference between plain old information and information to be used, and many argumentative mistakes throughout history were made because this difference wasn't considered. The difference is this: information doesn't exist, while information to be used does. And what that means is, instructions exist. There are no little factoids hanging about in the ether to be called upon at whim. No information stands on its own, devoid of context. Information is only ever information to be used. And language is rhetorical because the way information is phrased *is* the information to be used, it *is* the instruction.   Our words and actions are signals to others of how we should be addressed, and what should be addressed.   We choose our words according to what we think will best get people to follow the instruction.

We developed language in order to utilize others, to get them to do what we want them to do. That is what language does, why it comes about, and how it continues to live. It changes according to our needs and whims to utilize one another. Linguistically, language changes because our tongue is a muscle that flexes and relaxes, grows stronger and tires, and must conform to each particular mouth to produce the same sounds.   The common vocabulary changes as we abandon old connotations for new ones, as we explore our world a little more and as our needs change with the world, leaving holes that require words borrowed or created to fill them. Sometimes we ignore the holes entirely. Or sometimes a word becomes meaningless, but we continue using it anyway. Or as we stop enunciating the difference between one word and the next. As we learn new languages. And so on. Language evolves.

But rhetorically, language changes as conversations begin and continue, each participant making demands, each hearing the other's demands, and compromising. This continues until at least one person's demands are satisfied, or both give up. If one person's demands are satisfied, the rhetoric was effective. If both people give up, the rhetoric failed. Not coincidentally, in the case where rhetoric was effective, communication of meaning was successful. Language worked. In the case where rhetoric failed, communication of meaning failed. Language is, as I said, instructional.

Truth is a special feeling we get about certain sentences or their variations. This feeling is not immutable. It can be lost if you have it, gained if you don't, or doubted, or entertained. We tend to put our trust in the sentences that give us this feeling. That means, if you get people to feel truth where you want them to feel it, you control their trust. And if you control what it is they trust—well, that's a fortunate situation indeed, because you can get them to do anything you please so long as you maintain that control.

There is no Truth inherent to any sentence, there is only what people think sounds right. Anything can be argued. Everything is open for debate. And anything can be made to sound right. Now, this is not to say that you or I will ever have the talent to overturn extremely common and popular truths, such as:

"The sun is the continued source of all matter and energy on Earth."

"Barack Obama is the 44th president of the United States of America."

"You are reading this sentence."

"I know how to tie my shoe."

In general, the more widely accepted, popular, and pertinent a belief is to the daily lives of the masses, the more difficult it is to shift its truth. Surprisingly, the more personal a belief, the easier it is to shift its truth. Individuals are weaker than groups, after all. This is not to say that it is impossible to control the beliefs of a group. Group beliefs are constantly changing, at least as fast as language is changing. If you can push through and get a large audience to start changing their beliefs, the change is unstoppable. As a group, they tend to fight whatever is not the status quo in their group. But when a group is changing, that change *is* the status quo. Once the ball gets rolling, it gets easier and easier to roll.

The same is true for an individual, but less so. Individuals are narcissistic and self-centered. Instead of appealing to the status quo, you must appeal to what they think, what gives them that special feeling of truthfulness. What they think, no matter who they are, is still grounded in what is normal, but there's no actual "normal" here. What they think is grounded in an abstracted normal. To convince an individual, you must link what you profess to their beliefs in a way that makes the two appear the same or rely on each other. An individual has the ability to change their mind where a group can't, but as you'll see, this is much more difficult to do than simply fooling them into agreement. Either way, like groups, once you get the ball rolling, things move quickly.

While all language is rhetorical, not all rhetoric is argumentative, so Truth doesn't always play a role in language, and it is not what you will be manipulating. When a father tells his daughter she can't have another cookie and she gives "the puppy-dog eyes" and he finally gives in, this is effective rhetoric, not Truth. When a guy approaches a girl at the bar, strikes up a conversation, and she turns him down, that is ineffective rhetoric, not falseness. When a presidential candidate is voted into the presidency, this is because their rhetoric was effective. When an office employee asks a coworker to forward her a memo she lost, and the coworker says he will but doesn't, this is the result of ineffective rhetoric. When someone tells a joke and listeners laugh, it is effective rhetoric.

Talking is a whole lot like sex. Some people like it rough, some people like it soft and passionate. Some people want mutual contributions in a discussion, and some people want to dominate or be submissive. Some people need plenty of foreplay before the main event and some people just want you to spit on it, shove it in, and get to the point. And in all cases, if you blow your load too quickly or take too long, your partner probably won't remember your talk favorably. So you must always pay attention to the preferences of the person you're talking to and your audience and often forget your own needs in order to woo them.

Rhetoric is the use of language to please or persuade, as it's often defined. I said previously that all language is rhetorical, but in contrast to how it is often defined, not all rhetoric is lingual. Rhetoric pertains to how instructions are packaged, from the person saying the words, to the environment where the words are said, to the words themselves. The daughter's puppy-dog eyes are a rhetorical tactic. The man at the bar was probably turned down for more reasons than just what he said, including his appearance, the way he walked, how his voice sounded, how people reacted to him, etc. The presidential-candidate-turned-president won for many reasons, not just the language they used. The other candidate may have been deemed unelectable, and whatever means used to get that across was effective rhetoric. Perhaps the winning candidate was associated with someone repulsive to the public; if that association wasn't taken advantage of efficiently, effective rhetoric was not used. As far as the office employee is concerned, perhaps the coworker simply forgot. Nevertheless, effective rhetoric would be unforgettable and the memo would be forwarded. The person who tells a joke tries to get people to laugh, and in succeeding, uses effective rhetoric.

This book is not subtitled, "How to Use Rhetoric Effectively," but "How to Argue Effectively." However, there is no way to separate argumentation from rhetoric. If you're able to use puppy-dog eyes to convince a staunch atheist that God exists, or to persuade a conservative to vote for a liberal, you probably don't need this book. The line between argumentative rhetoric and non-argumentative rhetoric is not very clear. Generally, the goal of an argument is to persuade your opponent to your position. But your goal may be to discredit your opponent, or to simply piss them off. Or your goal may be to get people to laugh, or to cry, or to believe something that you don't believe. You may want to learn something, or want advice. Or perhaps you want to make friends or have a discussion. You may simply want to get your way. All of these are legitimate goals. You can tweak and apply the rhetorical techniques discussed in this book to many purposes. In learning how to get people to follow your hidden instructions a certain way, it doesn't take much abstraction to apply the methods elsewhere.

The instructions that sit in our language are ubiquitous. Each word you utter plays a role in delivering your instructions. I'll give you a real-life sample of this happening.

I stay up late at night, and I can be fairly loud. But because of the position of my desk in my apartment, my roommate could hear me down the hall even when I was quiet. With the way that sounds bounced off the walls, she could hear me typing at my computer. She complained about this, and so early one morning my wife and I discussed how we might reposition my desk. Our roommate came out and groggily said, "I can hear you guys talking about me." We insisted that we weren't saying anything bad, and she insisted again that she could hear us talking about her. We spent the day like that, going back and forth, insisting she could hear us talking about her, and insisting that we weren't saying anything bad. The matter was only resolved by carefully retracing our steps, and I learned that when my roommate said, "I could hear you guys talking about me," she meant, "I could hear you guys talking." That is, we woke her up again. Yes, it regarded her, so she wasn't incorrect, but to us it seemed like the superfluous "about me" was the issue. So we spent all day trying to correct the wrong problem. Correcting a problem was the purpose of both, "I heard you talking," and, "I heard you talking about me," but that little "about me" instructed us to fix a different problem than she wanted addressed.

And what of "I heard you guys talking"? How does that instruct us to fix a problem? Let's begin broadly. Descriptions introduce. Sometimes they introduce vocabulary; e.g., "God is all-powerful" introduces *all-powerful* into a discussion about God. Further descriptions of what *all-powerful* means introduce new vocabulary into a discussion about *all-powerful*, and, in this context, *God* as well.

When Sally gives a description of a crime, she is giving vocabulary about that crime. If Steve's description contradicts Sally's, he is introducing contradictory words into that discussion of the crime. The discussion that follows won't be descriptive of the crime (unless new descriptions are given) but semantic, arguing for or against the conflicting words. Sally wants the words "did it" to go next to references of Steve. Steve wants the words "didn't do it" to go next to references to him. They argue over what they can say. The goal is, at least, to get each other to say specific words. In describing, they not only introduced words, but also gave an instruction to use these specific words, and now they are both seeing their instructions through. There may be other instructions as well, such as performing an action. If Sally and Steve are in court, perhaps Sally wants Steve to pay a fee or go to jail. They both want the judge or jury to say they are right and the other person is wrong.

This is precisely what happened with my roommate. I thought she wanted me to apologize for talking about her. I wasn't talking badly about her, and saw no reason to apologize. To apologize could be taken as admittance that I *was* talking badly about her because, as far as I knew, this is what our fight was about. Come to find out, she wanted an apology, yes, but she wanted an apology for waking her up. Mostly, she wanted us not to wake her, one way or another.

Descriptions can also be an introduction of a

speaker, where the speaker describes the circumstances that compelled them to contribute to the discussion. For example, where I usually hear the phrase, "I heard you talking," is right before someone enters a discussion. "I heard you talking, and I think I can help." Other descriptions work like this as well: "Yesterday, as I was sitting on the toilet, it occurred to me..." "When I was a boy..." Sometimes, a description is an introduction of both a vocabulary and a speaker: "Editing was very difficult for me, but important. And that's why I think it's a good idea to have a few editors you know and get along with well." At the very least, all descriptions are instructions to allow a specific vocabulary into a discussion.

Now, if with "I heard you guys talking (about me)" my roommate was introducing herself into the discussion, we would expect her to continue. "I heard you guys talking, and I think you could move the desk over there." But that didn't happen. She did not enter into the discussion about moving my desk, so "I heard you guys talking" was the main thrust of her point. Statements are rarely made for their own sake (and even when they are, it's in the barbaric form philosophers use, having lost all sense of functional language and wallowing in dead words, like the people at the 8th circle of Hell in Dante Alighieri's <u>The Divine Comedy</u>, damned to seep in their own shit) so when someone says anything, they're hinting at something else related to the discussion. A child bursts into the room as their parents are talking about Christmas presents and says, "I heard you guys talking!" The hint is that the presents are no longer a surprise. Two friends are talking at a party, then they ask a third person for their expertise, and start summarizing what was already said when the third person says, "I heard you talking." The hint is there is no need to summarize the discussion. Two kids in the back pew of a church are talking while their mother is playing the organ. She comes back to her seat when the sermon starts and says to her kids, "I heard you guys talking." The hint is that they shouldn't have been so loud, or shouldn't have been talking at all.

What was my roommate also saying when she said, "I heard you guys talking"? What was the hint she gave? Similar to the last example with the kids in church, we shouldn't have been so loud. So even without the "about me" at the end, "I heard you guys talking" is an instruction, even though it's a description. And "I heard you guys talking about me," has even more possible instructions to it, because the "about me" could be superfluous, or not.

The tiniest semantic choices make all the

difference in what instruction is heard. Compare "He killed my father," and "He murdered my father." Though *killed* and *murdered* have very different meanings in a dictionary (while both words still pertain to someone ending the life of someone else), their applications are broad and the difference between them begins to blur. The normal dictionary use is clearly different: "He killed my father" doesn't necessarily imply that the killing was unlawful. Perhaps the father was a convicted murderer, and *he* who "killed my father" is the executioner. Perhaps the *he* and the *father* are both soldiers in opposing armies. "He murdered my father" in the dictionary sense doesn't have much ambiguity. The killing was unlawful. When you stray from that stereotypical meaning, the implications of these two sentences become interesting. What if someone said of the executioner, "He murdered my father"? The instruction is different. This person is trying to get us to see something moral about executing people. Or perhaps they are saying their father was innocent. Or perhaps their father didn't deserve such an extreme punishment. To push these use differences further into obscurity:

"Forty-five years of hard labor killed my father."

"Forty-five years of hard labor murdered my father."

"He killed my idea."

"He murdered my idea."

"Her jokes killed the crowd."

"Her jokes murdered the crowd."

As you see, the differences are subtle. But there are differences. And because of these differences, the listener will react and respond differently, though perhaps subtly as well. But that subtle difference in response could be the difference between, "Hmm... maybe, yeah," and, "Hmm... okay." To me, there's a huge difference between those two reactions, in that I like, "Hmm... okay," a lot more than I like, "Hmm... maybe, yeah." But I know that, to the speaker, there's usually not much difference between the two. (An interesting counter-example is in the term "serial killer." Why don't we call them "serial murderers," since that's what they are? By the strictest dictionary sense, any war hero with more than three enemy lives under their belt is a serial killer. Perhaps if we called the criminals "serial murderers," we wouldn't find such a fascination with people like Jack the Ripper, Ted Bundy, and Jeffrey Dahmer, but without the *k*-sound in *killer*, it almost doesn't sound extreme. Plus, *murderer* alone sounds very personal. *Killer* sounds like the person ends a lot of lives. *Murderer* sounds like the person ends *individual* lives. Many subtleties to think about.)

Anyway, now imagine differences in reactions that come from a sentence full of semantic choices.

"Her jokes killed the crowd."

"That comedian's routine murdered the audience."

Here you have not only the differences between *killed* and *murdered*, but also the difference between nearly all the words in both sentences. "That comedian" lends an air of authority to "her" that *her* just doesn't have. She's not just a pronoun, but a *comedian*. And I used *that* to refer to the comedian, rather than *the*, which gives a sense of pointedness and direction that *the* doesn't have. However, compared to a word like *a*, even *the* lends an air of significance. So it's not just the comedian, but *that* comedian. Quite a different thing.

Then there's *jokes* and *routine*. Again, *routine* has an authority that *jokes* doesn't have. Anyone could tell a joke, but not everyone has a routine. It is not ordinary, and it feels more practiced. (Again, keep in mind that *jokes* and *routine* refer to the same thing.) So, "That comedian's routine," means the same as, "Her jokes."

Skip *killed* and *murdered* since we covered those and we come to *crowd* and *audience*. "The crowd" seems disorganized, almost coincidental, compared to "the audience." There's also a sense of ownership in "the audience," like it's not just a bunch of people, but *her* bunch of people. (I momentarily thought of putting "her audience" rather than "the audience" to change all the words in the sentence, but because of that subtle sense of ownership already implicit in "the audience," I thought it was redundant. Plus, if I had, it would have been harder to see the ownership already implied in "the audience.")

All these differences in word choice mean a different reaction from the listener—in general, "That comedian's routine murdered the audience," demands a more severe reaction, and probably favorable. I imagine it is harder to brush off or keep a muted composure than hearing, "Her jokes killed the crowd," the way I would brush off someone's unexcited assessment of a movie: "How was the movie?"

"It was good. I liked it."

Nod.

I've gone a bit off-track. The point is to show you the instructions that fuel our words, and how we can fail ourselves if we aren't careful to choose the right words, rather than the words nearby. Saying, "I dispute that," is harsher than, "I question that," and you should only use one or the other when the word's tone is most advantageous. Saying, "She is wrong," is different than saying, "She is not right." There is semantic choice in all of our words, and learning to control it gives you an edge against your opponent. But we'll discuss semantic choice later. For now, it is enough to know the basis for semantic choice, the instructions embedded in our words.

The object of the game of argument, the whole point of rhetoric (and really, the whole point of talking), is getting what you want. You win if you get what you want. Simple.

If you injure yourself and you want help or sympathy, or if someone is at fault and you want them to feel guilty, say and do the appropriate things to get that help or sympathy.

You've fallen and skinned your knee. A friend is standing next to you. If you want your friend to help you ease the pain, complain that it really hurts. Reach out your hand. Exaggerate a limp. Ask for their help. Of course, you won't need to do any of these things if injuring yourself, itself, is why they helped you out. If you want them to feel guilty for hurting you, even if they aren't at fault, ask them why they hurt you. Or level insults at them for hurting you. If they don't feel at fault for your injury they may protest, but keep at it. Arguments don't last forever, and you don't have to convince them that they were at fault to win—you must get them to behave as if they feel guilty. Try a passive-aggressive approach; pretend that you've given up the argument by saying, "Fine, whatever," but make sure they know you still think it's their fault. Avoid looking at them while maintaining an angry face, and make sure they see it. If they try talking to you, turn your shoulder. If they insist again that they weren't at fault, perhaps saying that you are behaving outrageously, say something like, "Why are you talking to me? I already said, 'Fine, whatever.' Why do you care how I act, all of a sudden? If you really don't think it was your fault, then stop trying to argue that it wasn't your fault. It just looks like you're making excuses for not saying you're sorry." If that doesn't get them to apologize, continue your passive aggressiveness. If they do apologize but still divert blame, such as, "Well, I'm sorry even though it wasn't my fault," or, "I'm sorry that you hurt yourself," be snarky. Say, "Oh, that makes it all better," and continue your passive aggressiveness. But don't push it too far. Battles over vocabulary and instruction are resolved with compromise, and sometimes it's necessary that compromises take place. If they apologize but you detect a hint of insincerity in their voice, ignore the insincerity and assume that they meant it. Treat it as if it was exactly what you needed to continue your friendship. An authentic-sounding apology is, after all, the indication you needed that they feel guilty, and thus, your goal is accomplished.

This brings up an important issue of what you *can* want, what *can* possibly count as winning. No matter how hard you try, you'll never know what goes on in a person's mind. You have only what they say and how they behave to judge by, so it's only by what they say and how they behave that getting what you want is determined. Of course, if you'd like to make someone's private thoughts the object of your desire, I won't stop you. I think my approach speaks for itself in practice, and you won't be in danger of endlessly searching for proof that someone actually thinks one way or the other.

Go back to the skinned-knee scenario. Instead of seeking an apology, what happens if you want the person to be genuinely, sincerely sorry? Suppose you receive an apology with no hint of sarcasm. Since it's not their actions or what they say that you're after, but their sincerity, do you accept or reject their apology as sincere? If you reject it, at what point will you accept it? If you accept it, why not accept the apology as sincere back when the apology had a hint of insincerity (assuming that what a person says and how they behave *aren't* what you're after)? When your friend gives an authentic-sounding apology, demanding more authenticity will only wear on their nerves. If it is your *goal* to receive multiple apologies, you need to understand that people require conditioning for anything that is not already normal for them. If this is their first time apologizing to you, there is no precedent for how to satisfy you. You must get them to apologize more than once to begin that trend, but to get the least amount of resistance, you should probably stop at two or three. They won't be happy about apologizing more than once, but they'll get over it. The next time they're in an apologetic situation, try to elicit one more apology than the first time, and one more than that the next time, and the next time, and so on until they lose count of the number of times they've had to apologize.

Now, this example of the use of rhetoric in an ordinary situation may not be the robust connotation of argument that comes to mind when we think of formal debate, so you may wonder if winning is the same in formal debate. The answer is yes. (We will explore tactics in further detail later, and whether some tactics are appropriate for all arguments.) There are a number of different kinds of formal debate, each depending on the goal of the debaters, as the goal is what the format is designed around. Generally, formal debates consist of two opposing sides of an issue, each represented by a person or team, and an audience. Some debates have either side trying to garner support from the audience. Some have each side trying to persuade the other. Some aren't even about persuasion or raising support at the expense of the other person, but about displaying tactics to judges, like a dog at a dog show. Or working together to expand on an idea or solve a problem.   Winning in each kind of debate means achieving the goals of the debate.

No matter what your goal is, control over the vocabulary is your primary objective. Whoever controls the vocabulary controls the debate. This fact is something Americans in particular learned during the Bush administration. Thanks to my nemesis, Frank Luntz, that brilliant bastard, neoconservatives ruled the world for 12 years. (I call him my nemesis because we do the same thing for different reasons. By contrast, I call Noam Chomsky my enemy because we do different things for the same reasons. Luntz is a corporate whore—though I'll grant that he *can* be. I am not a corporate whore. I can't be. There's no corporate market for me. If there was, I'd probably be a corporate whore too. At any rate, I beg you to supplement this self-published book with his best-selling book, <u>Words</u>

<u>That Work: It's Not What You Say, It's What People</u>
<u>Hear</u>. It's good. Brilliant bastard.) Luntz polled people to see what sorts of words and phrases made people react favorably to the neoconservative agenda, and then he sold that information to neoconservative politicians. The neoconservative politicians took that information and applied it according to the methods developed by Leo Strauss, the father of neoconservativism. The method is this: describe a situation by identifying the "bad guys," and repeat as often as possible. They would simplify a situation in terms of good and evil, placing themselves squarely on the side of good, and their opponent evil. Frank Luntz's information was put to use in defining their opposition as evil. For a well-known example, the neoconservatives spent some time trying to destroy the estate tax, the tax you pay when you inherit valuable things. Luntz asked

himself, "Since you pay this tax when someone dies, how would people react if we called it 'the death tax'?" Polling showed an overwhelming number of people automatically hated that tax, when moments ago they didn't mind the estate tax. Calling it "the death tax" made people think our rotten government was out of hand and willing to tax anything. And a new evil was born. The estate tax was then called the death tax whenever a neoconservative talked about it. It was repeated and engrained in people's minds, and thousands of people called their elected representatives and demanded we stop taxing death. All because someone had the brilliant idea to change the vocabulary we use.

Back in the 1930's, a man named C.K. Ogden developed a simplified version of English, called Basic English, that he hoped everyone could learn, and would be used as an international language. It is still used as a tool for teaching the English language. At the time, George Orwell loved the idea, but as World War II started and Nazi propaganda spread over Europe, Orwell changed his mind about Basic English. Hitler was seducing the German masses with Nazi propaganda, the principles of which he argued in <u>Mein Kampf</u>. I quote, "It is a mistake to make propaganda many-sided, like scientific instruction, for instance." And later, "The function of propaganda is, for example, not to weigh and ponder the rights of different people, but exclusively to emphasize the one right which it has set out to argue for. Its task is not to make an objective study of the truth, insofar as it favors the enemy, and then set it before the masses with academic fairness; its task is to serve our own right, always and unflinchingly." Lastly, the US Office of Strategic Services outlined Hitler's tactics as such:

"Never allow the public to cool off; never admit a fault or wrong; never concede that there may be some good in your enemy; never leave room for alternatives; never accept blame; concentrate on one enemy at a time and blame him for everything that goes wrong; people will believe a big lie sooner than a little one; and if you repeat it frequently enough people will sooner or later believe it." All these have to do with controlling and limiting the language people use. Orwell paid close attention to Nazi propaganda, and came to see in Basic English the very key to enslaving people. When he wrote about this in <u>Nineteen Eighty-Four</u>, he called it *Newspeak*. And the people that enforce the use of Newspeak are called "Thought Police." To stray from *Newspeak* is a "thought crime." For George Orwell, I think we can safely deduce that he thought to control vocabulary was to control the way people think of things. The more limited the vocabulary, the harder it is to disagree.

(To take one more shot at Luntz, in his book he points out that the term "Orwellian" is associated with double-speak. He goes as far as to say that the language developed by the government in <u>Nineteen Eighty-Four</u> was called *Doublespeak*. It's *Newspeak*. *Newspeak* doesn't allow double-speak, by anyone, because it limits semantic choice. Without common synonyms and double-entendres, not even the totalitarian government could speak duplicitously, because the people didn't know any words that *could* be duplicitous. Orwell would rather duplicity in language than limitations in language. The scene in Room 101 doesn't have Winston Smith learning duplicitous language—it has him learning to limit his language. Duplicity empowers, limitation enslaves. Luntz bemoans how "Orwellian" came to mean what

Orwell was against—double-speak—and says that he is Orwellian in the sense that he agrees with Orwell. He should have simply pointed out Orwell's argument for a richly nuanced language, pointed at his own work as a prime example of exploring nuance, and been done with it instead of complaining using arguments so easy to criticize.)

I'm not one to confuse genocide with overturning tax laws just because the same tactic was used in their support. The tactic is not evil. I called Frank Luntz my nemesis, but I think the work he does is genius. His methods are not evil. I hope you understand why I encourage you to use the tactics of the Nazis and of the neoconservatives. They will help you win arguments, and that's as far as I'll encourage you—I'll have no part of what you do with that tactic. This tactic applies to everything, including "scientific instruction." An argument doesn't have to be two-dimensional for you to require control of the vocabulary to win. The debate between general relativity and quantum mechanics in physics, for example, ended (in that those who agreed with general relativity exclusively more or less gave up) when quantum physicists developed new language to describe the movement of particles. It's no longer seen as "spooky." (There was also plenty of testing to go along with it, but it's not a coincidence that these tests and the new language arose at the same time.)

I have Susan Mazzoni to thank for showing me this next little exercise used to activate prior knowledge to enhance children's reading comprehension. It's a simple version of the techniques that we literate people use unthinkingly to read. She told me, "Here's a word from the story we're going to read."

The piece of paper said *baseball*.

"Now, what do you think our story is going to be about? What do you think will happen in the story?"

I said that it could be about someone who plays baseball.

"Could it be about anything else?" she asked.

I said maybe it was someone who wants to play baseball. Or someone whose hero is a baseball player. Or perhaps it's about a kid who accidently broke a window with a baseball.

Susan took out another card that said *greatest*.

"Now what do you think the story is about?"

I said it could be about the greatest baseball player ever. Or it could be the greatest baseball game ever. Or it could be about how baseball is the greatest sport ever.

She took out a third card that said *practice*.

I said it must be about how much practice it

took to become the greatest baseball player. Or how someone realized baseball is the greatest game ever while practicing. Or when a baseball coach told his team, "That was the greatest practice ever," emphasizing that practice can make coaches prouder than a game, teaching kids a valuable lesson.

"Last one," she said, and pulled out a fourth card that said *Babe*.

And I ran through the possibilities, all including the name of Babe Ruth. She pointed out that a child doing this exercise might be inclined to say the story was about *baseball, greatest, practice,* and *baby,* but the capital *B* in *Babe*, signifies that it's a proper noun.

The point of the exercise is to get me to recognize and use the given words in various ways and then together as the context is changed by each new word, and even with capitalization. The child takes a proactive role in engaging language, developing a deeper, fuller grasp of language through the exact same processes we go through in the split moment between reading this word and the next. But for our purposes, it can be used to show the way in which we appeal to the given vocabulary. *Baseball* is given, and in processing what it could mean, I used it. Then, when *greatest* was presented, I used both words to hypothesize what could be going on. Then again for *practice*, and so on. Try this exercise with a friend to see for yourself how we appeal to the given vocabulary.

So get control of the vocabulary because it puts you in control of where the argument will go. It's a lot easier to criticize a death tax than an estate tax, and that criticism can only happen if you introduce it and convince people that it's the right word.

There are no rules. This doesn't mean your audience or opponent won't play by them. It certainly doesn't mean you shouldn't pretend to play by them. They can be useful. For example, the other day my wife asked me about the unfamiliar phone number listed numerous times on our phone bill, and why I was coming home late so often. Now, don't you go assuming the worst. There's a very simple explanation for all of this, which is that I am having an affair. Of course, it's my wife I'm talking to, and I really don't need her invading my personal life, so I need to change the topic. Language compels people to stay on topic, and if I tell the truth, there's no reason to think she won't stay on topic. I don't want that. So do I lie? Do I hit her? Do I pretend like I'm having a heart attack? Any one of these would stop her talking about my affair.

Hitting her is the obvious answer. The initial shock of being hit will keep her silent for a while. But there are a few problems with hitting her. If I haven't hit her before, hitting her now might just confirm her suspicions and cause her to ask more questions about my affair. This harkens back to what I said about conditioning people. Plus, these days, hitting my wife may get me into trouble with certain liberal activist groups, like the police. So even if the precedent has been set that I hit my wife whenever she says something I don't want to talk about, hitting her may not be the most effective approach in the long run.

Should I lie to her? There are a number of ways I can do this, and I'll probably end up using several ways at once. For example, to lie about coming home late, I could say I was doing something that I won't get in trouble for doing. I could blame someone else for my tardiness. I could say that I haven't been late, and it's just her imagination. But will this keep her from talking about it? As long as she doesn't know I'm lying, or at least as long as she knows I'm lying but doesn't think talking about it more will help her feel better, the topic won't come up again. And there are things I can do to maintain her trust in my lie, such as not being noticeably inconsistent, using facts and lies that support my main lie, and get people to serve as a witness and lie for me. Faking a heart attack is a lie, but not one that will keep her trust for long. I don't need to explain why.

Speaking of consistency, consistently arguing effectively requires a fair amount of consistency of character (again, harkening back to my point about conditioning). You don't actually need to be consistent; you only need to appear so. Is the blue that I see the same as the blue that you see when you look at the sky? Who knows. Who cares. But it appears so because we both say *blue* when we need to say the color of the sky, and that's all we need to effectively say what the color the sky is. The same goes for what you think and the way you feel. Is what someone thinks you think the same as what you think you think? Maybe not. What matters is that you appear to think what they think you think. That is consistency of character. You are welcome to appear inconsistent, but don't come crying to me if that doesn't work out when your wife asks you why you're late and reeking of sex.

At any rate, there are no rules. But there is winning and losing, so there are better approaches than others. So, rather than discuss rules, we'll discuss some good, effective strategies for winning.

Dishonesty is something you'll be accused of by people who want to think they're better than you for following norms of discussion. It's very much like being crude. You'll only ever be accused of crudeness by people who think they're better than you for being polite or using proper etiquette. Honesty is a myth, just as etiquette is a myth. Both are standards people pretend to live by, imposed by society, which is person upon person holding each other up to those standards. There is no standard of honesty hanging about in the ether. There is no god that will shock you with a tiny lightning bolt every time you lie. There is no greater good you must help along, but if there is, you're one person, and no matter how important people think you are, you're insignificant to it. In less than five billion years, Earth won't exist, and neither will anyone that could remember you were a little sneaky with your words. Any greater good we could come up with is not great enough to overcome that fact.

There is an obvious stigma attached to the word *dishonest*. We think of outright lying, even though there are many subtle aspects of dishonesty. This is why, in the movie, *The Invention of Lying,* people don't only tell the truth when they say something, they say everything that comes to mind. There is nothing hidden. If they could hide something, then they should be able to not tell the whole truth, and we, the viewers, would sit there wondering why these people hadn't figured out how to lie.

I tell my wife I love her, and I do this often. It is true that I love her. But that's not the only reason I remind her of this. Sometimes I do it to ease her stress. She sometimes gets flustered when the tiniest thing goes wrong, and in these times, I tell her I love her to remind her that not everything has gone wrong.

I also enjoy, when she's not stressed, the way she turns and looks and smiles at me when I tell her I love her. Sometimes I tell her I love her just to see her turn and smile. I don't say why I'm telling her I love her, because that would dampen the effect. So there is a hidden agenda to telling her I love her in these situations. That's not lying, but it's not completely honest either, in the same way that, when my wife asks where I've been and I say that I was at work but leave out the bit where I was fucking my boss, I'm not *lying* but I have left out some information on purpose. Dishonesty. But there's also a sense in which intention isn't necessary. When my boss calls me and asks what I'm wearing, I tell her, "Nothing." That's not actually true. I still have my wedding ring on. I forgot about it completely. And most people would—it's not like we'd call wearing nothing but a wedding ring "being clothed." But it's also not the whole truth, and in that sense, it's dishonest.

Let's get something straight. I don't condone outright lying, unless it's a really good idea. And it's not a really good idea very often. It's just too hard to keep lies straight and convincing. And most of the more dishonest tactics are very effective in moderation. The big reason dishonesty is discouraged is because people frown upon it, and when you're trying to get people to do what you want them to do, frowns show reluctance, and reluctance is just two blocks east of refusal. Appearing honest isn't a rule, just a very good suggestion.

The best sort of dishonesty I know, the kind that

I use the most often and is most useful, is double-standards. You won't want to make these apparent; you want half to publicly thrust the audience in your favor, while the other half is your own little tactical secret. For example, I like to call people manipulative, and show just how they're being manipulative. Perhaps they're choosing loaded words. Or perhaps they're choosing normal words that I want people to think are loaded because they hurt my case. I do this to manipulate onlookers to resent my opponent. Who wants to be manipulated? Nobody. Everybody wants control of their own thoughts, and they'll rebel against anyone they think is trying to manipulate them. You'll note that, publicly, I'm taking the honest side, while privately taking the dishonest side. There's nothing wrong with this. Everyone does this automatically. It comes easy with ideologies. Do you think we should keep the world clean? I'll bet you don't pick up every piece of trash on the sidewalk. Don't you hate people that talk on their cell phones while driving? I'll bet you're guilty of the same thing. (Oh, sure, *you're* the one that still drives well while on the phone.) Think the Holocaust was a terrible thing? What are you doing about genocide that is happening *right now?* You're reading a book. But I'm sure you'll get right on that as soon as you're done.

Double-standards can't be helped. If there's one contribution the postmodernists made to philosophy, it's the extensive work they did to show the unavoidable hypocrisy in everything we do. Don't try to get around it. Just embrace it and be as aware of every hypocritical thing you do as you can. My favorite example of people who are ignorant of their hypocrisy was in a commercial made by The Truth, the anti-smoking lobbyist group. To show how ridiculous smoking really is, they had a guy offer to let you suck on his car's exhaust pipe for the price of a pack of cigarettes. The idea was, since it's stupid to suck on a tail pipe, and cigarette smoke has a lot in common with exhaust fumes, it's stupid to suck on a cigarette. A potent message. But it does leave us to ask, "How much damage do cars do to us, then? Shouldn't we have stupid commercials telling us that driving cars is evil? Where are all the anti-car lobbyist groups, especially considering that driving is a much more popular habit than smoking?" We could go on and ask what the statistics are of people dying from second-hand exhaust, and why there are no such statistics, or why people aren't given a no-exhaust lane on the highway, but we won't. That'd be ridiculous, right? I mean, right? And there we have a perfectly good example of how badly things can go because of our hypocritical nature. They used cars to show that cigarettes are stupid, even though they drive cars, and I turned that right around to show that since exhaust bans that resemble smoking bans are ridiculous, the smoking bans are ridiculous. Sure, it may not be entirely convincing, but it certainly dilutes anti-smoking propaganda— people might be passionate beforehand, but faced with a little hypocrisy they weren't previously aware of, their enthusiasm loses steam. And anyone who doesn't let on that their passion isn't quite as forceful is labeled a fanatic, not persuaded by new data, but driven by an agenda. Any grandiosity they held is stripped away in the eyes of the audience, and they'll hang themselves if they keep talking.

I would now like to take a moment to give you some very good advice: if you have ideologies, if you have standards, if you have beliefs (you probably have all three), get rid of them. They'll only hold you down. They are your weak spot, because you're incapable of seeing how they make you a hypocrite.   You can't see them as hypocritical—they're right. They are all you see and they are your blind spot, all at once.

This is the second kind of dishonesty I recommend, because it is dishonest in a way to enter into an argument with no allegiances. The late, great Chaim Perelman wrote, "We must not forget that by listening to someone we display a willingness to eventually accept his point of view." (1969, page 17.) I agree with this. I agree that we put our beliefs on the line when we speak to one another, whether we like it or not. And that is why I recommend you not have any beliefs. While you display a willingness to eventually accept their point of view and give up your own, you don't actually need to have a point of view to give up.

(I need a tangent. Grant me a tangent. My tangent is this: When I say do not have any beliefs, I don't mean just common beliefs, like believing in ghosts or God or some abstract and wholly dubious notion of freedom. I also mean thinking that one position is better to have than another. This tangent is specifically targeted at the new crop of atheists that Richard Dawkins, Sam Harris, Christopher Hitchens, and the like have given us. When you think you don't have a belief, you're mistaken. At the very least, you believe you're right. Okay, okay, you *know* you're right. Your manufactured knowledge is a burden to your effectiveness. If you don't want a blind spot, you'll do away with childish things like that phone book you're standing on to make yourself taller. You're not fooling anybody.)

So how do you avoid tying yourself down with allegiances? And wouldn't that prevent you from arguing at all? You can't actually get rid of your allegiances—like I said, everything we do is hypocritical, and this cannot be helped—but you can hide them so well that it would take a postmodernist to drag them out of you. Start by not having "your position." All you need in order to argue is a contrary position. Instead of providing your own contrary position, let your opponent give it to you. Suppose you are one of the new crop of atheists that I tangented at. Instead of bringing your atheism to the table when you debate a theist, simply be what the theist is not. Then you can take advantage of their hypocrisies without having to defend your own, since your hypocrisies were created by them, and are therefore their hypocrisies as well. Suddenly you're blameless. How did that happen?

But resist the temptation to simply argue everything, or people will write you off as the contrarian bastard that you are. If you pick your battles according to what you actually agree or disagree with, people will view you as someone with specific goals and aspirations and ideals, even though you never depend on them in an argument. If you are an atheist, argue with theists. If you are a republican, argue with democrats. And so on. Being forced to oppose these people in order to debate eliminates the need to bring a definite stance to the table.

Much of what people hold true relies on what they think "everyone else" thinks is true. This abstract notion of "everyone else" is the fulcrum of all arguments. It is the first audience, and it is always there. But there is no actual "everyone else," it is simply a construct. We justify our actions through it: "Everyone else is doing it." "Everyone else says so." "Everyone gets this but you."

this but you."

Each of us validates our ideas through "everyone else," even when we are going against the status quo. We recognize when we are rebelling because it's not "what everyone else is after." When "everyone else" is too oppressive, we act out against them. We say, "I don't care what everyone else thinks."

Depending on how your audience feels about

"everyone else" in a given situation, you can manipulate them by arguing that "everyone else" does or does not endorse a position. You see, we humans are not empirical creatures. We are egotistical, and we align ourselves with the nearest friendly face (then, if we're wrong, they take the blame) to protect our egos.

But be warned: you have vulnerable allegiances with "everyone else" as well. You cannot rid yourself of them, so don't try. The most you can do is be aware of them, list them off in your mind, and keep track of them. Then at least you will know when they are being used against you. You may then go on to decide when you want to keep those alliances with "everyone else."

Having a sense of social norms is necessary for any language speaker. Even when "everyone else" is a single person, perhaps the very person you are speaking to, norms are what lend a sense of continuity to the meanings of words. This is what makes language seem like it's never changing, even though it is, both linguistically and rhetorically, all the time. So even at this fairly fundamental level of continuity of meaning, each of us has a sense of "everyone else." However, never assume that is the only way which you are vulnerable. As I continue through this chapter, watch how I use "everyone else" against you.

How "everyone else" is viewed will depend a great deal upon the settings for your argument. For example, if your audience is a single person and you are alone, explicit invocation of "everyone else" may not be effective, or necessary, because it is more obvious that "everyone else" is not around to confirm what they think. Often, using "everybody else" in a one-on-one discussion is downright dubious. Then again, these matters are contextual, depending entirely on the situation, and it may be effective to call upon "everyone else" as an authority.

There are many variations of audiences. Usually, arguments and audiences are divided into four categories, although the lines between them are rather blurred: one-to-one, one-to-many, many-to-many, and many-to-one. I think it's more helpful to think of these as grammars or ways to talk to people, rather than actual categories of audiences.

One-to-one arguments are those like I described earlier, where you are arguing with a single person, and no one else is listening. If there are people listening who are not contributing to the argument, whether you have a one-to-one or a one-to-many argument will depend on your goal. If your primary goal is to persuade your opponent, then you have a one-to-one argument. If your primary goal is to persuade the people who listen but don't contribute, then you have a one-to-many argument. (Of course in that case you actually have a one-to-one-to-many argument, but as I said, this is how it is traditionally categorized, and traditions rarely have anything to do with practicality, save for following the status quo.) When you speak to people as if it were a one-to-one argument, it tends to make your audience feel like the talk is more personal, that you are perhaps sharing something with them that you wouldn't normally share with people. This brings trustworthiness, and as you recall, trust is exactly what you are after to change people's beliefs. I am, for example, speaking to you in this way right now.

You see one-to-many arguments quite often on television, where a speaker is addressing the viewers, or when a preacher stands at the podium and speaks to his congregation. Generally speaking, avoid this grammar. It presumes an elevated status over your audience. Televisions and podiums are platforms that come with connotations of elevated status, and there aren't many other places that do. Unless you are actually on TV or standing at that podium, you probably do not have the necessary support from your audience to come off as anything but elitist, thinking you're better than "everyone else."

Many-to-many arguments are seen in the democratic process, or when organizations attack groups of people or other organizations, or when protesters are divided on the streets. Here, the public eye ("everyone else") plays an important role. Usually, the goal is to garner support from undecided onlookers. That support may then be used as leverage to get the other group to stop what they're doing, either of their own free will or through legislation. (Legislation is preferable as it ensures that it won't happen again. If legislation isn't possible but the other group does agree to cease and desist, there forms a precedent. If it happens again, the first organization can point at the prior agreement to stop. After all, what would "everyone else" think if the second organization was shown to be hypocritical?) Using a many-to-many grammar to a single person leads them to feel like there's something bigger to be part of. Likewise, it makes them feel like they aren't yet part of anything. This is useful because nobody really wants to be a loner if they can help it, and it's much easier to get them to join the nearest group. However, if the many-to-many grammar is used with a person that does not want to agree with you, or wants nothing to do with you, it may serve to polarize them against you. And they do so with the blessing of "everyone else."

Many-to-one arguments are a rather new

phenomenon, only common since the development of the Internet. Before then, the closest form of many-to-one arguments was polls. On blogs, videos, products, etc. people leave comments, voicing their praise, insults, agreements, disagreements, and elaborations to the authors of these web pages. Of course, these are individuals addressing individuals, but some very valuable insight can be gained from thinking of the situation in various ways. For example, someone creates a video and posts it to the Internet: if most of the viewers (in the eyes of the video creator) voice their disdain, then the video creator is bound to think the video is a failure, even if there are a few people that praise it. "Everyone hates it," the creator thinks.

Many-to-one grammar is, I think, the greatest and potentially most effective rhetorical tool mankind has ever known. Suppose you organize a group of people to spread a message of failure to a number of individuals: if you present yourselves and speak as if it's a many-to-one argument (though it is actually closer to a many-to-many argument), the victim automatically feels isolated, singled out for failure. If you speak as if the argument is many-to-many, the individual automatically feels associated with "everyone else," even though that does not include you and your group. That is, you've empowered that individual.

There is no automatically correct way to view and address your audience. You will simply need to continually judge how they want to be treated, in what ways they will allow themselves to be talked to, and do your best to stay within those bounds as you try to get what you want.

Boredom is your enemy. It doesn't matter how good or bad your argument may be, how right or wrong your opponent: If people can't pay attention, they can't hear you. And because they're quite aware that *you* are what is boring them, they're bound to have some ill-feelings toward you. Nobody wants to be bored, and therefore, nobody wants what bores them. And since you're boring them with your stance, nobody wants your stance. You lose. It's as simple as that.

There's a reason you'll find joke books in the speech-writing section of your local bookstore. There's a reason starting off your speech or presentation with a joke is a stereotype, especially in the business world where people who have never spoken in front of a crowd are often thrust in front of their coworkers to tell them how some new doodad or doohickey works. Their managers think this enables and empowers them. I think it just sets them up for a whole lot of embarrassment—the anticipation of which motivates them to drive to that local bookstore, look in the speech-writing section, and pick up a joke book. The reason you'll find joke books there is because a whole lot of people found out they are boring when they speak.

In these cheesy business motivation, self-help books (and they are cheesy, I don't care how much it helped you self-help yourself), they will inevitably advise you to use jokes because they break the tension and get your audience interested. This is only partially true at best, but there's a better reason nobody ever talks about. If these books did tell you the real reason jokes are important, fewer people would feel helpless and, even after the jokes, embarrassed as they laugh way too loudly at their own joke, which usually had almost nothing to do with the rest of the presentation. The joke gets groans or nothing at all, people cross their arms and tune out whatever comes next.

What comes next is, simply put, not a joke. Don't think this goes away for someone comfortable with public speaking, and whose jokes are right on topic. We can infer from our business-motivation self-help books that a presentation will not break the ice, ease tension, and interest listeners. Well, why not? I think the primary reason anyone becomes boring is that they don't enjoy their words. The subject shouldn't matter (though enjoying the subject matter certainly motivates us to be more concerned with our words); if you love the words you use, relish them and allow yourself to be captivated by them, what's left for people to dislike? Oh, sure, plenty of things. But let's look at how a love of words changes the way people react.

When a storyteller speaks, even when not telling a story, they captivate listeners by giving a sense of movement to their words through suspense. You are sucked through each sentence, word by word, and if there's a pause, you wait anxiously to hear the next. They can take a description of the mundane and make you yearn for more. They do this by leaving out enough information in their words that you must keep listening to get everything. But they also give you just enough information so you aren't confused as to why you're listening. It's a tightrope they walk without effort. Or so it seems. It actually takes quite an effort. It involves speeding up and slowing down the rate at which words come out, and inflecting appropriately—perhaps a little hushed here, then louder, more excited here. Fast, now slow

77

and leaning in, and then straightening up—they speak conversationally with you. Back to excited and hurried! And so on. They take such an interest in their words that they take the time to *live* the words with their gestures, their inflections. (This is actually a misconception about acting. The goal of an actor isn't to be natural as we all are on a daily basis. The goal is to be interesting in a way that looks like it took no effort at all. When there's no perceptible effort to be another person, it seems like the actor *is* that person.) Now, this performance may not be funny, but it's certainly engaging. And that tension you feel when you stand up in front of people is probably just you. If you're speaking to your coworkers, I'll bet nobody cares enough to be tense. And if I'm wrong, tension is nothing an engaging talk can't handle.

There are countless ways to love your words. I'd talk about all of them, but—they're countless. So you'll just have to settle for something near the next best thing, which is examining a few of them. I never did get around to telling you the real reason jokes are important to speeches and presentations, and argumentation and rhetoric as a whole. I'll do that next.

Laughter is the real reason jokes are important. Even for that poor newcomer to public speaking that laughs nervously at his own jokes. Laughter comforts us, at least when we're the ones laughing. The coworkers might not find the speaker's nervous laughter very comforting, the way the Joker's maniacal laughter doesn't comfort Batman. But laughing, even when something isn't funny, is a comfort mechanism. The effect is exponential when a group of people laugh together. Laughing by ourselves may be a way for us to relate to our predicament, but laughing together is a way for us to relate both to the predicament and to each other. And relatability is your best friend.

Suppose you're in a formal debate. Your opponent is a little playful, and while he's making all his points, the audience is roaring with laughter. You make your points just as well, but you're not trying to be funny (because *that's* completely inappropriate in a formal debate, *of course*), so the audience is dead silent.

Look at this scenario and keep in mind that you don't know what the debate is about and what positions you and your opponent are taking. Who do you think is winning? Do you think the moderator or judges aren't swayed by your opponent's charm? You're both making your points succinctly, providing evidence and decent arguments. But your opponent is murdering you. Not killing. Murdering.

Laughter is a form of agreement. How many people who think we have a responsibility to recycle and use renewable resources aren't swayed by George Carlin's "The Planet is Fine"? Some people might object that they were *swayed*, but instead were *charmed* by that routine. You can call it whatever you want, but if you call it anything other than being swayed or convinced I'll quietly call you a liar with my eyes. See my eyes? They're saying, "Liar," all accusatively-like.

But seriously, you are a liar. You were swayed. He made you criticize yourself with your laughter. It wasn't just that it was funny; laughter was your coping mechanism. We think of comedians as not serious—not just *funny* as opposed to serious, but *absurd* as opposed to serious. George Carlin wasn't being absurd at all. He made some very valid points: the world *will* be here long after we're gone, no matter how much we litter, no matter how many otters die in oil spills, no matter how much oxygen is left when there are no rain forests. The world doesn't care that we trash our home—*we* do. We *are* being self-important when we say the world needs saving—*we* need saving. It's not only funny when he says it, it's a good point. But is that point as well-taken when we hear that loud, know-it-all uncle say it at family reunions? Of course not. What was it Mary Poppins said? "A medicine full of sugar helps the spoonerisms go down"? Something like that.

Whether you want to call it *swayed* or *charmed*, your laughter aligned yourself with him. For perhaps the briefest of moments and in the remotest of ways, you shared something. You thought the same way. Or you wouldn't have laughed. It's as simple as that. Think about it: what's the structure of a joke? You've got the setup or the story, and then you've got the punch line.   What's the punch line?   It's the unexpected conclusion of the story. But it's not so unexpected that it makes no sense. It just makes a different sense than we were expecting. "Two guys walk into a bar." The setup. We've heard jokes about guys walking into bars before. And then the punch line: "The third one ducks." It's not nonsense, just a different sense. A different sense of the word *bar* than we were expecting. When we laugh at that (okay, okay, pretend you laughed at it), this is our coping mechanism for being taken by surprise, and we must in that same instant regain our balance in this new sense to understand what's being said. You see? Agreement. Sway. Not just charm.

There is another way laughter comes in handy: it makes people forget. Slightly relevant jokes make terrific tangents that will lead people's attention off-topic. What happens after a good laugh is people forget exactly what was said and will settle for a summary to put them back on track. As long as you're the one making the summary, you control where the conversation goes. The little bit of sway that laughter brings will push people right into your arms. And your summary, of course, supports your point rather than your opponent's because, of course, it's your summary. Laughter is like a reset button on the back of everyone's head. Use it to make your case on a clean slate.

When it comes to being funny, put down the joke book, or you'll be talking about that third guy that ducked at the bar, like I just did. Learn to entertain and get laughs from comedians themselves. Find one you like, and study them. Why do you laugh when they say this? Analyze it. Then start practicing. Try those same methods in your day-to-day life. When someone asks how your day was, try to do what your favorite comedian does. It won't work at first, so learn to be okay with embarrassment. But keep trying, because it takes a lot of practice. Comedians spend their whole lives perfecting style. You just started, and it's an ongoing process. And hey, in the end, humor just might not fit you. You're at a disadvantage, but you'll manage. Laughter isn't *everything* in argumentation.

Language has many mediums. There are, as far as I know, three main categories of language: spoken, written, and body language. Depending on what kind of audience you're communicating with, each of these categories has countless mediums. For example, in spoken language, there is conversation for when you're speaking one-to-one, speech performances for when you're speaking one-to-many, chants and slogans for when you're speaking many-to-many or many-to one, etc. All mediums have their advantages and disadvantages, and you can understand these best by looking at the disadvantages of one medium through the advantages of another. For example, writing has an advantage over speech when it comes to specifics and how much information is packed into each word. When people read, they can look over statistics and then reread them to understand the sense they make. They can even come back much later to fit things together or remember what was said. If you try to do the same while speaking, giving a lot of specifics, you'll lose your listeners in a heartbeat. Complicated data was only invented after writing. Imagine Romans building the Coliseum without blueprints. Imagine James Joyce reciting <u>Ulysses</u> to his publishers instead of sending a manuscript. Imagine Andrew Wiles proving Fermat's Last Theorem for the first time in front of an audience without a chalkboard. Imagine that you had to make your computer do what does by saying, "One," or, "Zero," instead of having the binary coded into it.

Think about how bored you were at the last high school graduation ceremony you attended. Each and every graduating student must be called out. How many of those names do you remember? Probably only one, especially if the graduation wasn't yours. And if it was, you probably don't remember the names as they were called out, but rather, you remember who graduated with you. That's what happens in speech. People remember a summary of speech.

"Our neighbors came to talk to me today."

"Oh yeah? What'd they say?"

"They said you should stop dancing naked in front of the windows."

The neighbors probably said more. In fact, we automatically assume they said more, and that this is a summary. There is no, "Hello," which was probably said before the neighbor started complaining. There is no introduction to the problem, no rhetorical tact, which would inevitably be there when bringing up such an embarrassing topic. And so on. If we asked this person to remember the whole conversation with the neighbors, they might be able to give a very close approximation, but they'd certainly struggle to do it. (And I'd argue it is impossible to repeat exactly what was said once the conversation was over. How many *ums* and *uhs* and stutters and corrections and restarted sentences, which happen for everybody at an average of one disturbance every 4.4 seconds of talking, could they put in the right place?) These are details, and we don't retain details when we talk.

We can take advantage of this disadvantage of speech. If you are in an argument and people are watching, you can bring the onlookers to your side by leading your opponent into specifics. Everyone will get bored of what they're saying, and wait anxiously for you to talk. Now, there is a tiny obstacle to overcome here, and that is we are conditioned to think that anyone that can make our eyes glaze over and our hearing go fuzzy must be intelligent and credible. But that doesn't mean we like them. This tactic won't win the argument for you, but it will make people more receptive to you. (But like almost anything, moderation is best. Do this too many times and you'll establish your opponent as the person who would know because they have all the facts, and yourself as the person who doesn't know, so you ask a lot of questions to find a hole that you can finally attack.) In turn, you will need to use generalized data. This is why when you hear numbers on the news, it's usually in nice, rounded numbers like "one-thousand" or "7 billion." Your opponent will probably use generalized information if they know anything about speaking in front of people. As I said before, let your opponent determine who you are. To discredit your opponent's generalized information, you need to find a way to tastefully demand specifics.

"The dinosaurs died 65 million years ago."

"Yes. Today marks the 65 millionth anniversary of the extinction of the dinosaurs. As of 65 million years ago yesterday, they were frolicking in the flowers, eating each other, and singing songs with children for public television."

Retaliation like this draws everyone's attention to the incredibly vast generalization "65 million years" really is. If your opponent doesn't take the hint to be more specific, keep cracking jokes or asking for more specific data. If they still don't, they'll look like they're hiding something, or that their position is only supported by vague data, and would fall apart under any real scrutiny. And if they ever do start reciting lists of facts, they'll bore the audience.

That's one way of taking advantage of that disadvantage of speech. Be sure to always use a medium's advantages to your advantage, and a medium's disadvantages to your opponent's disadvantage. I'll list some of the advantages and disadvantages of mediums.

Writing is a solitary act. There is no immediate feedback, and so the writer never knows quite how well people understand them. Even if you sit in front of the writer and read so you can ask questions and argue as you go, it's like engaging two different people—the ink on the paper can't hear you, and the writer isn't who is making the points, they just know a lot about the argument. Writing also forces you into an intimate setting with language, which is good for the writer because they have the opportunity to make the best sentences to capture their ideas, but it's bad for the reader because not many people want to be intimate with someone else's language. Reading isn't as natural to us as listening. When we read, we must force ourselves to keep going, as if the act of reading, itself, is a distraction from what is written. But having obtained a commitment from a reader to keep going, you can write much, much more than you could ever speak while keeping people's attention. Part of the reason for this is it doesn't usually take people as long to read a given number of words as it does to listen to the same number of words. Another part of the reason is that we can reread what is written, so it's difficult to lose our place for very long. Writing also requires no performance as the words go on. Nobody hears me speak these words unenthusiastically. Nobody is looking at my body language. No one sees me picking my nose as I write this sentence. (Okay, I wasn't picking my nose as I wrote that, but I am now.) So in that sense, writing requires less effort. And you can edit your writing. If you misspeak in writing, use the backspace key. Writing happens without regard for time, so in the same way that readers can reread, writers can rewrite. Lastly, writings have no inherent voice. When we read, we impose a voice, and that voice has its own inflections and mannerisms. It is not the voice of the writer. This could be helpful, or it could be detrimental. If people impose a voice they made up, it makes the text potentially more personal than speech could ever be. A good writer makes us feel like what we're reading was written just for us. But people imposing a voice means that the text is more ambiguous and subject to the whims of the reader and how they wish to interpret. So our point might be lost for an entirely different point.

The characteristics of writing are very much in contrast to speaking. Speaking is public; it's done with other people and their immediate reactions. So while you can't go back in time to edlt, you can redirect yourself according to your listener's reactions. Also, while there aren't many different ways to be alone, as you are in writing, there are many different ways to engage listeners. Much of this was covered when we talked about different kinds of audience. There are some people that can speak to an audience for hours. You can't do that while having a conversation or debate. People expect to hear more than one person talk, and they become annoyed if one person talks for a long time—something to keep in mind if you're faced with an opponent who talks a lot.

Another advantage of speaking is that listening is second nature to people. They've been doing it since they were born, and they've been making sense of what they hear since before they could speak. The voice they hear is yours, which means there is not as much potential for as personal a touch. But for this reason it is also much, much harder to misinterpret (though it still happens) because there is less ambiguity through inflections, intonations, and stresses.

Engaging people through speech requires more than just your voice. If people sense you're insincere because you show no emotion while speaking of something emotional, they'll write you off. If your body language and inflections are downright boring, nobody will listen. On the other hand, if you act out your words well, your point will be that much more exciting and that much more moving, in a way that writing could never achieve.

There is also the matter of stutters, slips, and stumbles. We cannot get rid of them. They play a vital role in communication. But writing doesn't have them, and for some reason or another, people think we shouldn't have them in speech as well. You *can* take advantage of this, but be very, very careful. If you accuse someone of not fully convincing themselves of their own argument because they stuttered a little, people will certainly agree with you. But pointing it out raises the audience's awareness of our verbal blunders, and you're bound to get caught in your own stutter. In fact, you'll probably make yourself so nervous and self-conscious that you'll stutter even more. The same goes for pedantics in grammar. If you correct someone's grammar, not only is it obviously off-topic, but you're bound to use some improper grammar yourself. Hell, the wonderful and delightful language I'm using right now was created through people speaking improperly. And no language is free of a similar history. What will you do if, after you correct your opponent's grammar, they correct your grammar by saying that you're supposed to pronounce the *-ed* in past tense words, the way we do in *coveted*? The pronounced *-ed* was saved in most of the words that ended with *t* or *d*, or if it was used primarily in the language of the upper-class and academia, but it was lost in most other words. When it started to happen, people would write *lov'd* and *weigh'd* and *hear'd* to indicate how the word was said phonetically. Imagine someone saying, "I hear-ed you," these days. So no, there is no proper way to speak, and if you insist there is, a very embarrassing moment will come when you are shown to be not only a hypocrite, but a pedant of trivialities.

And just so that last paragraph isn't completely off-topic, writing is a major factor in slowing changes to spoken language when there is wide-spread literacy. But that does require your audience to be literate. Spoken language has the advantage that you can take it anywhere.

99

Say as little as possible. You can always say more. You can't say less.

It was very tempting to leave this chapter at that, but I don't mean by, "You can't say less," that you should say fewer things, that you should give less content. I mean that you should have as much content as necessary to be understood, using the fewest possible words. If, after writing a sentence with the minimum number of words, it would look or sound or resonate better with another word or two, go for it. Just don't be a whore, using every fucking word that comes to mind. Nobody listens to whores.

A sentence is like a party. Too few words and the party is over before it began. Too many and there will be words that sulk in the corner and won't have anything to do with anyone else. There will be plenty of third-wheels, those people that hang around two people that are trying to have a meaningful moment. There will be unnecessary repetitions, so that John can't decide between Tina or Sally, since they're so similar, and because John can't decide by the end of the party, nobody's getting laid. There will be loud-mouthed people that everyone wishes would go away. And there will be enough people that didn't pay attention to the invitation that the whole theme of the party is lost. The key to a good party is to have just enough people, each with distinct personalities, that everyone carries their own weight yet feels included and important. That's the sort of party people will talk about for years. Mark Twain wrote down eighteen rules for writing, and number fourteen was, "Eschew surplusage," which is the shortest way to say in English, "Get rid of extra words." And as the greatest writer in the English language, Mark

Twain knows best.

But there's another way in which we should be mindful of extravagances, and that is in our syllables and the sounds we make, which are called phonemes, and the commonality of words. The easier something is to say and remember, the more likely it is to be repeated. "Get rid of extra words," though it has one more syllable, is something you can take anywhere. There are variations that would match the syllable count of "eschew surplusage," like, "Leave off extra words," or, "Delete extra words," the latter of which has only one more word than Twain's, but "leave off" might not ubiquitously mean "get rid of," and *delete* has the distinct connotation of writing on a computer, when we need something that will apply to speech as well. So I think we can sacrifice the minimal syllable count of those two options in favor of "Get rid of extra words."

If you don't mind, I'd like to resurrect George Carlin again. Carlin had a great bit about euphemisms where he walked us through the history of what was called "shell shock" in the First World War, to what was called "post-traumatic stress disorder" by 1980. And through the history of what we called this condition, you can see the words soften, pile up, add syllables and, by the end, a hyphen. He makes the argument that we water down these words with syllables and extravagant new clinical terms to soften the impact a person's problems have on the people around them. We don't want to deal with old people, so we call them senior citizens. The effect extra syllables and words have on us is we stop listening. Now, this isn't necessarily a bad thing. It can certainly get you out of a jam in a jiffy. Politicians use it all the time so that nobody can accuse them of not saying anything, but it also loses all impact it might have. I remember when Larry King asked Representative Michelle Bachman if she thought people who say Barack Obama wasn't born in the United States (called *birthers*) were nutty. She clearly wanted to say, "No," but for some reason that one-word sentence came out, "You know, it's so interesting, this whole 'birther' issue hasn't even been one that has ever been brought up to me by my constituents. They continually ask me, Larry, 'Where's the jobs? I want to know, where are the jobs?'" Perhaps this was her attempt to bring up a subject with which she could bludgeon people. I don't know. (And who could? I lived in her district until recently and I never had my complaints heard, nor have I ever seen an ounce of improvement.) It failed, whatever it was. But if you're any better at rhetoric than Michelle Bachman, you can probably use this tactic successfully. However, I'm of the mind that obscuring things through lingual extravagance is better criticized than used. While we might think a person smart for making our ears go numb with big words, in the end, the person that says it best is right.

But there is a definite sense in which my alternative of "Get rid of extra words," fails. *Surplusage* doesn't only mean words and their syllables. It also means punctuation, tangents, clauses, prepositional phrases, and so on, where "get rid of extra words" really only means words, and no other part of our sentences. Think about it: punctuation causes us to pause when we see a comma or period, to raise our voice for the last part of a sentence when we see a question mark, to fake enthusiasm when we see an exclamation mark, to stutter when we see an ellipsis, semi-colon, or em dash. Too much punctuation overloads us with considerations. We end up paying more attention to what we're supposed to do than we pay to the message.

And this is yet another lesson we learn from Twain's, "Eschew surplusage": Context will play its role. He didn't need to specify that he meant words, syllables, and punctuation, or specify that he didn't mean to include wearing too much make-up or producing more of a product than demand will buy. "Eschew surplusage" was number fourteen of eighteen rules of writing. It would be odd if anyone read that and assumed he meant we should get rid of that subscription to that magazine we never read, or that we should cut back on drinking, or stop having children because eight is enough. Ironically, *words* in "get rid of extra words," is surplusage, because context would have clued you in that I'm talking about words, had I let it. Context is your friend. If you need to say more, you always can, but you can't say less.

I said earlier that consistency of character is important to people, and now I'm going to negate that a little. Contradiction is not a bad thing. Humans are conflicted. Everyone has opposing views on something. If you can show reason to hold contradictory ideas, it will make you more human, and thus, more relatable. They will think the issue is obviously something you care a lot about. And not only that, but you must also know enough to doubt your own position. Don't be wishy-washy about it, like a lover in a love-triangle in a bad opera. Be direct and sound like you know exactly why this is a difficult decision (even if you have yet to think of why). And then, appear to know enough to start leaning further and further toward the position you're taking. If you can then break free of the contradiction—with what looks like a lot of effort of course—and come to rest on one side or another, people will follow by the hoards.

A word of caution: this act is *not* a simple pros and cons list. I've seen people get up on a stage and actually do this, as if it convinces anyone that they're conflicted or actually considering the other side of the argument. It looks rehearsed and dull. And as soon as you are boring, you'll lose. In fact, avoid pros and cons lists altogether. Your opponent should be defining you. You should not be defining your opponent.

No, what you want is a dramatization of your struggle with the subject. The more it looks like you're actually having that struggle right there in front of them, the more brilliant, interesting, genuine, and convincing you'll be. In this way you *do* define your opponent, but not in any way that your opponent can object to, because it seems like this is all you.

Rather, what happens next is your opponent will try to use the good things you said about their position by tweaking them into a more acceptable version. Here is where you start making demands on vocabulary, which your opponent will grant you in your emotional state. If they resist, outright reject them. It's something people do when we're looking for answers but can't find any that satisfy. We turn flippant in frustration. If they do nothing, go through your schpiel of internal conflict again, but more quickly this time, and obviously favoring your conclusion. This shows passion and conviction, and even though nothing new is really said, you are starting a precedent that will make it even harder to tear you down. In my experience, people bow out of debates at this point. It's like, when my wife is crabby and I compliment her, but she takes the compliment as some slight against her.   For example, I once told her I thought she was attractive, and she insisted that I meant she was fat.   Or the time I told her that I love the way she sings and she insisted that I thought she was a terrible singer. Or the time I asked if I could get her anything, and she insisted I was calling her a lazy slob. There is no way you'll get me to press on with the compliment and force her to take it.   I can't win in those situations. And neither can your opponent.

There is another way contradiction is useful, and that is, when you embrace one, you're only ever half wrong. That's a funny thing to say, but it's also useful. If you can obscure the contradiction enough so that no one recognizes it as a contradiction, it allows you to choose which way you want to go at a later time (when you can propose another contradiction, if you want). I'm thinking specifically of those moments that your opponent forces you to take some initiative. You're supposed to be reacting, letting your opponent define you, and there will be times when they insist you stop simply opposing what they say and take a stand of your own that they can oppose and be defined by. If you use an obfuscated contradiction successfully, they will take a stance opposing what they think is your position. You are then allowed to oppose them again, to be defined by them again, because they had to assume *something* in order to think you took a non-contradictory stance.

Now, a time will come when you are confronted on your contradictions. It happens to the best of us, and it'll certainly happen as you begin exploring what they contribute to an argument. Don't be discouraged. First, there's no law against using contradictions. Calling you on them is just someone's way to try to get you to submit to conventions of argument. I'll bet most of the people won't be able to answer this question: "So what?" They might say, "It means you're wrong." You can object to this. The thing about arguments against contradictions is that they rely on "common sense." There is a point at which they will ask you to look at something, and you are under no obligation to recognize it. For example, someone might say, "Contradictions negate themselves."

"They also support themselves."

"But they make your point pointless."

"So what?"

"So why should I listen to you at all?"

"That's a good question, but you decided to listen to me before you found out I endorse a contradiction. Nothing has changed in me. But you've changed now that you think I'm not worth listening to. So a better question is, why should I listen to you? You're just going to change your mind whenever things don't go your way."

"You should listen because I don't use contradictions."

"I'd like to believe you, but you might change your mind, and then I'd be the only one that agrees with you, since you wouldn't even agree with yourself. Ironic, isn't it, that you'd be contradictory? But I suppose at least then you'll be consistent, instead of changing your mind like this."

"But I didn't change my mind."

"Oh, then you'll have me for an argument, contradictions and all. Good."

"No, I won't. Contradictions make no sense."

"How so?"

"Look at them!"

"What about them?"

"Well, just look!"

What just happened is someone being forced to appeal to an area of common sense that's so common, we don't even have language to address it. As long as you can give onlookers a reason to think that your opponent should be able to answer for their appeal to common sense and take responsibility for it, it will seem to them that your opponent doesn't know what they're talking about.

But suppose your opponent can speak their reasons for distrusting contradictions. This will happen every now and again, because there are people out there that are better versed in these things than you, and you won't be able to make your way with clever wordplay or by turning things around on them. Just remember that contradictions happen all the time in ordinary, everyday language, and nobody bats an eyelash because it makes sense.

We usually do this when we can't find the right word. "What's that word I'm looking for? It's like an example, but it's not." That's a contradiction that could prove very useful in helping you find the right word. Sometimes we use a contradiction *not* when we are trying to find a word, but when there still isn't ample language, and we don't mind that. "Getting this job was the absolute best thing that's ever happened to me. It's also the absolute worst thing that's happened to me." There's nothing confusing about that. Contradictions are normal and useful in that they show us something in a place where there are no good words. Now, since you're already in a position where your opponent seems smarter than you, play the dumb card. Don't be stupid, but play your contradiction off as an example of you trying to come up with something where there is no better language. Your opponent may try to guess, but you don't need to let them guess right. Or they may ask you to elaborate, but you don't have to. Tell them, "Maybe I didn't make this clear enough two sentences ago. There is no better language, because there is no established language for what I'm after." This not only validates your contradiction, but it makes your opponent look stupid, and if they were able to bring you to this far into a debate about contradictions in the first place, they need to be knocked down a few notches.

All second-hand information is acceptable on the authority of another person. That is what makes it second-hand, after all. And how we interpret all first-hand information is through the authority of another person as well. (For those that would disagree: at the very least, interpretation is a matter of language, and language is taught to you by other people.) In other words, authority is very important to accepting information. When someone tells you something, you only accept it as far as you trust them to know what they're talking about, as far as you consider them an authority on that information. So getting that authority is essential to winning an audience, and your opponent.

Credibility would also work here. Credibility and authority are usually synonyms. But I would say that credibility is only *most* of what authority is. Authority is more than just the credibility you have; authority demands that people listen. Credibility is what makes people believe. A person may seem credible, and so we are inclined to believe them. But if a person seems authoritative, we feel compelled to listen. —This difference between believing and listening, aside from the difference that credibility *suggests* while authority *demands*, is crucial because while we might be automatically inclined to believe someone, that doesn't mean we'll necessarily hear what they want us to believe. Credibility is a big part of authority, but authority should be your goal. Again, your authority should include credibility, but you need that voice, that composure, that confidence that commands people to pay attention.

Getting that authority when you don't have it is difficult. People are ruthlessly protective of their allegiances because they don't want to be or look misinformed. The kind of authority you see in information and argumentation is very much analogous to the lawful kind of authority you see in government or management. How many people want more bosses to look over their shoulder, or more governments with more taxes and more laws? How many people would rather be their own boss, their own leader, their own inspiration, their own source of information? Nobody will believe everything they hear, and how they decide who they listen to is by judging not only the argument itself, but the person arguing, and the people to whom they deflect responsibility for the information they're using. People resist new authorities no matter how good they are. Authorities must prove themselves, but since they're usually not around, you need to prove them. (You have to prove yourself as well—this is why I keep giving you different ways of gaining favor with your audience.) So here's how to do that.

The first way is simply to give someone credible-sounding information with a name attached. You could say, "My friend Joe said it's going to rain tomorrow." Now you don't bear the burden of the information alone, even though Joe is nowhere nearby. But this won't always work. The weather isn't something that people argue too often, and doesn't hold a dear place in many people's hearts (which is an interesting point in itself: not only do we tend to argue things we're a little bit passionate about, but the act of arguing a topic makes the topic dearer than it was). "My friend Joe says that Jews secretly offer their children as human sacrifices, just as Abraham did with Isaac." This isn't something you and Joe can carry on your own very well. So we need to add more authority. We can do this in two ways: first, we can reveal that Joe has recognizable expertise in the field of Jewish human sacrifice. Joe could be a Jew himself, or an anthropologist of Jewish culture, or a scholar of secret Jewish texts. But Joe might not be any of these things, so we could either lie and say he is, or we could divert the responsibility of the information to yet another person. "My friend Joe was reading an article by a Jewish scholar of secret Jewish texts in an anthropology journal that said Jews secretly offer their children up as human sacrifices, just as Abraham did with Isaac." This too might be an outright lie, nevertheless we've reached a point where, while our opponent might disagree, they can't simply dismiss it because they have to dismiss you, Joe, the Jewish scholar of secret Jewish texts, *and* the anthropology journal. Instead, your opponent will take careful steps to discredit the authority of each and every one of you. First, you and Joe. They will ask to see the paper. If you can't show them where to go read this article, this discredits your authority in that you are gullible and irresponsible in choosing which authorities to rely upon. This also discredits Joe because the paper doesn't appear to exist, when he said it does.

But suppose you can produce the article. Your opponent's next step is to discredit the Jewish scholar and the anthropology journal. If the article contains flimsy reasoning and very little evidence, then it will be difficult for you to defend (and you would need to defend it, since your credibility is still in question. That doesn't end just because you showed them the article. The whole thing still relies on you and Joe, in that order, because you brought it up as a contribution to the debate). But because you depended on Joe for the article, you can admit it's not good evidence and maintain your authority by blaming Joe, who gave it to you. Admitting you were misinformed will damage your credibility slightly in regards to who you trust, but it will also increase your trustworthiness as someone who doesn't insist they're right when everybody has an excellent reason to believe otherwise.

But suppose the article was just fine and meets the scientific standards your opponent requires. Your opponent has to build up a collection of information and authorities, and then your information and authorities will fight against theirs, through the two of you. The idea is to strengthen your authorities with more information, or to bring in more authorities, or discredit your opponent's authorities. When doing this, I warn you to err on the side of fewer authorities. That may seem counter-intuitive because the more authorities you call upon, the more authorities your opponent must attack. But the fewer people your audience has to keep track of, the further engrained each name will be, and consequently, the more credible each name will be. Then again, if it works better to bombard people with authorities to the point where they must submit, even if it's because they don't want to run the risk of looking stupid because they couldn't keep up, go for it. But again, rhetorical authority is much like political authority. If you have too much authority, people will up and revolt.

The second way to prove your authority's worth is through its associations. Suppose we said, "My friend Joe, who is a graduate student at Yale University, told me about an article written in the most popular and critically acclaimed anthropology journal in the history of the field, by a Jewish scholar of secret Jewish texts, who won a Nobel Peace Prize for his work saving Jewish children, that said that Jews secretly offer their children up as human sacrifices, just as Abraham offered up Isaac." The scenario would play out the same, but it's certainly a new dimension of authority. These are mostly authorities through establishments. There is also an authority through expertise, and even fields of work and study. When someone questions whether Richard Dawkins is actually a scientist, they're seeking to discredit him by finding a lack of authority by expertise, work, and study.

A third way to bolster support for your authorities is to link them to the authorities of your opponent or of your crowd. This does not mean that you pit them against one another. Instead you use them to build each other up. If I could find a way to link Joe to my opponent's friend, Bill, then it's harder to deny Joe his authority because my opponent must also deny the authority of Bill, and through association, some of their own authority. Be wary, though, because your opponent will obtain the same credibility for Bill as we gained for Joe. That's the way associations work: if you compare something your opponent says to something really bad, it doesn't just downplay what your opponent says, but elevates the really bad thing. For example, there's a big controversy going on right now where people are comparing Barack Obama to Adolf Hitler because they both had agendas to socialize some services. It *is* something they have in common. But they don't have much else in common, namely the genocidal rampages. The genocide and all around evil of Hitler is what separates him from Obama. Yet, because they are being compared at all, it brings down Obama. What sane people are up in arms about is that Hitler's deeds must be taken so lightly in order to compare him to Obama, even when it comes to something they actually have in common, like socializing agendas. The semantic choice of calling Obama the same as Hitler demands that we think of Obama as bad as Hitler, and Hitler as good as Obama. Obama is brought down, yes, but Hitler has risen to not-so-evil. Remember this when using this third technique, because you may not want your authorities to be on an even playing field. This is a tactic mostly reserved for when you're losing the argument, or when your authorities aren't trusted as much as your opponent's. (And if you catch your opponent doing this, feel free to point that out to them.)

Authority isn't reserved for people. I've been building up Joe, but I could have been building up an ideology, tradition, or information. In ancient Greece, before Socrates, people considered sophistry an illustrious practice. Thanks to Socrates, Plato, Aristotle, and nearly every single person in the Western philosophical tradition, sophism has lost its authority as something trustworthy. To call someone a sophist is to bring them down to the level of authority that sophism now has. To call a philosophical movement like deconstructionism *sophistry* is to do the same. Contrariwise, rationalism has enjoyed a long and happy existence in western philosophy in its many manifestations, and thanks to that, to call something *rational* is to give it the authority of rationalism. Same goes for logic and *logical*, though it wasn't long ago that being logical took a back seat to being faithful, religiously speaking. Associations and authorities come and go because of the constant ebb and flow of their negative and positive associations with other authorities.

The last thing I'd like to comment on is appeals to authority as "fallacies." I don't believe in fallacies, and this "fallacy" isn't an exception. People appeal to authority all the time. What they're complaining about is the presumption that a person, organization, or ideology should be automatically authoritative. I mostly agree with this. Authority is something to earn, not demand. But, as always, if you can get away with it, please do, because you've been allowed a shortcut to winning the argument.

To debate an ideology, you must explore extremes. People can interpret normal, everyday life any number of ways, according to any ideology, viewed through any paranoid delusion, and never encounter conflict. But what is an extreme? Extremes are rare circumstances that mark ideological boundaries. They are exceptional circumstances. But often they are circumstances so broad, universal, and trivial that they are overlooked because they aren't brought up in normal, everyday life. And they are only called *extreme* by the mouth of the ideology itself. So really, extremes are just any possible exception. Here's a simple example from The Secret, written by self-help guru Rhonda Byrne, called the *Law of Attraction*: you can change your circumstances by changing your attitude. If you generally think negatively, you'll find yourself in generally negative circumstances. If you generally think positively, you'll find yourself in generally positive circumstances. Now, I put this into terms where it is less severe than often presented. In The Secret, Byrne explicitly states that it isn't just generally changing your circumstances, and it's not just generally thinking negatively or positively. She insists that wishing very hard for something specific will get you that specific something.

In everyday life, our desires are usually small. "I want to have a day off." "I'd like more money." "I'd love to tap that ass." And so on. The cozy thing about ideological principles like the Law of Attraction is that no matter whether the law controls a situation or not, we can interpret the situation through it. If someone gets more money, proponents of The Secret will say, "You see? That person wished hard enough for money that they got it." And if someone hasn't gotten more money, they say, "You see? That person needs to wish more, concentrate and focus better." And when it comes to the outrageous things we want—to live forever, to be the richest person in the world, to marry Angelina Jolie (a feat which not even Brad Pitt accomplished)—the fact that we don't have them means that we don't want them badly enough or we don't believe we can have them. No matter what happens, what goes right or what stays wrong, the Law of Attraction is still true. The least crazy version of the idea is, when you wish hard enough, you at least subconsciously change the way you live in order to acquire what you want. The Secret is not of the least crazy kind. It would have you think that you have a telekinetic link to the universe that physically brings you what you want. And as crazy as that is, we won't find exceptions in ordinary examples of getting or not getting what we want. We must go to the extraordinary examples for possible exceptions. This is why Hitler and the Nazis are used in so many arguments about ideologies: they're an extreme example in a number of ways.

Now, the sort of extreme we need to look for is someone not getting what they want even though they want it badly enough. The opposite of this is someone that gets something even though they don't want it. Examples where the something the person didn't want was good rather than bad, doesn't offer any help because, well, the something was good, and who are we to complain? But where someone gets something they don't want, and that something is bad, is basically the same as someone not getting what they want—they got what they didn't want. Therefore, someone not getting what they want must be our route to defeating the Law of Attraction.

I don't want (and so I'll never get!) just a single exception, I want to bring down the whole mess, so I need to find the broadest extreme I can muster. And I think I've found one. Survival. Survival is something everything living wants, which is pretty broad. (And arguing that not every living thing wants to live is beside the point.) Survival is the mechanism by which we evolved. Characteristics arise and change, and are the fulcrum of survival. The Law of Attraction, a law of the universe, applies to everything that *can* want. The thing is, living creatures utilize all the laws of the universe they can to survive. As a law of the universe, you'd think everything would survive, since it's not only what every living thing wants, it's necessary. Survival is the very core of their being. You'd think we'd all utilize this law just as we utilize all the other laws in our own ways. The fact that it isn't second nature to every living thing to utilize the Law of Attraction makes no sense. We utilize gravity to walk, and that's second nature. Assuming the Law of Attraction is correct, if we want it enough, we shouldn't need to walk to get anywhere. It's potentially the most efficient means of transportation ever. Somebody call GM—I've got a design for a new car that uses an alternative fuel: unleaded wanting-it-bad. You know how badly people want that fuel when you look at how much they're willing to pay for fossil fuels. That should pull GM out of bankruptcy. And the fact that we don't all survive makes no sense either, as we're built around surviving well. It's a desire we all know how to do. Wanting to survive is the bottom-line. There is no wanting something more or better or more efficiently or with more focus than we want to survive, and the Law of Attraction fails to give us what we want. And don't tell me we survive through our children. Even if that was true, there are plenty of evolutionary dead-ends, where there is no next step in the lineage of the species. They're just gone, and it's not because they wanted to go. And thank goodness for that. They make up our fossil fuels. In the end, it's ironic how The Secret *wants* a Law of Attraction, but doesn't get one.

And there you have it, a staggering blow to the Law of Attraction as The Secret presents it by undermining its core. We wouldn't have a persuasive argument against it without exploring extremes, the land of exceptions, where rules and unfaltering truth fray like the ends of a rope. Use extremes to take down any ideology, morality, or assumption that stands in your way. The bigger the extreme, the better—like taking an anti-aircraft rifle to a squirrel. You won't need a taxidermist.

There are people that think extremes are useless. Ayn Rand, another self-help guru, author of The Fountainhead and Atlas Shrugged, was one of them. And also of course her legions of drones, the Objectivists, which is funny because whenever someone tried to object to her, she called them irrational, untruthful, and not serious. Certainly, an ego to be reckoned with. She disallowed extremes as counter-examples particularly concerning her moral philosophy. She thought people should be selfish, and all evil comes from altruism. But we can't explore how right she is and where she starts to be wrong because we can't use extremes. And we can't use extremes because—she says so? Fuck that.

When Ayn Rand says selfishness is goodness, she doesn't mean any old selfishness. We must be rational in our selfishness. We can't just be whimsically selfish. We can't for example deny people their rights for our own good. This avoids accusations of hedonism. As far as this much is concerned, we could play with the inevitability of hedonism in humans. Rand says that what a living thing *is* determines what it ought to do, and as rational creatures with a history of self-interest, we should therefore *be* rationally self-interested, as if existence or life was not the morally ambiguous bystander we think it is. Existence and life are not, in other words, *potentially* good. They *are* good. Or at least they can be good. So they ought to be good, because being good is somehow a more complete use of our talents. Humans came to be who we are in an evolutionary history of taking what isn't ours, of denying others their rights, of hedonism, and yes, sometimes of "rational" self-interest. But the rational self-interest we employed was only "rational" in that it met her standards of "rational self-interest" by accident, not through any reasoning process. We weren't always the robust creatures we find ourselves to be now, and who we were, even as a different species, is very much part of who we are now. So why suddenly should we not consider our history, which is the only thing that *could* make life unambiguous, just as the words I've already said make the words I'm saying now unambiguous? We are capable of thinking, and so we should think—but we're capable of all sorts of things, good and bad, by any standards. We are not inherently good, nor are we inherently bad. Rand, rather inconsistently, agrees with this when she says: "Life is given to [man], survival is not. His body is given to him, its sustenance is not. His mind is given to him, its content is not." To soothe the inconsistency, perhaps Rand could have added, "Morality is given to him, knowing about it is not," or "… the choice to be moral is not," or something like that. But since knowing the difference between good and evil or choosing to behave morally are not things we are born with, *being* moral is not part of who we are, and so not what we necessarily *ought* to be. So, since we are not good-doers or evil-doers, what we *ought* to do is not concern ourselves with morality. Or maybe we ought to just ignore Ayn Rand when she prattles on about it.

What I've done here is take an extreme, which is the boundary of our existence as rational, thinking creatures called humans, and linked it to our unthinking ancestors and our irrational births. Then I supported it with pertinent quotes from the horse's mouth, and thereby juxtaposed our current selves against our former selves to create a conflict in the ideological framework Ayn Rand gave us. If I am not permitted to explore extremes, I could not make this criticism. So it's rather convenient for her that (she argued) we can't use extremes. She argued that extremes, being abstractions and hypotheticals, are not "objective," as far as she demanded we use the word *objective*. But here again we can use her words against her by juxtaposing them with an extreme. The sort of thinking that separates us from the beasts, the sort of thinking that is rational, is highly abstract (and therefore not objective)—even little things we take for granted all the time, concepts like *tomorrow*. Nonobjective thinking makes us what we are. It appears that Rand would have us deny what we are when it suits her, and embrace it when it suits her, too. No, by her own reasoning, what we are is a thinking sort of creature, and so we ought to think. We shouldn't deny ourselves some thoughts just because some lunatic woman said to. Use extremes whenever you need them, and don't bother with frugality. Don't miss out on an opportunity to win just because you felt some pressure to keep your use of extremes to a minimum.

Never feel obligated to adhere completely to reality with your words. A little surreality never hurt anybody. In fact, you'll need it if you ever want to crack a joke—reality has no punch line. Surreal explanations, descriptions, tangents, especially when people know it is intentional, lightens moods and makes people playful.

There are two ways to embrace surreality and make it work for you. The first is negatively, juxtaposed against reality. You take a surreal situation and present it as reality to show just how absurd that surreal situation is, since people will recognize it as not-reality. We call this *sarcasm*, and it's a wonderful tool because you're allowed to play with your opponent's argument to discredit it, rather than just outright attacking it. It turns your opponents against themselves if they disagree with it. And they will be tempted to disagree with it at the very least because *you* are making the argument, and not them. One of my favorite little romps through sarcasm is Captain Stormfield's Visit to Heaven, by Mark Twain. It's a short story about a man who dies, has all these expectations about Heaven, and at first, his expectations were right. Then, time passes, and we realize just how long eternity is. So does Captain Stormfield, and he starts to look for other things to do. The story is, broadly speaking, a sarcastic representation of things that elevate our sense of self-importance. Not only do we end up questioning our ideas of Heaven, but also our place in the universe, as there are different heavens for alien species on all sorts of planets. One of my favorite passages is this:

Between you and me, it does gravel me, the

cool way people from those monster worlds outside our system snub our little world, and even our system. Of course we think a good deal of Jupiter, because our world is only a potato to it, for size; but then there are worlds in other systems that Jupiter isn't even a mustard-seed to—like the planet Goobra, for instance, which you couldn't squeeze inside the orbit of Halley's comet without straining the rivets. Tourists from Goobra (I mean parties that lived and died there—natives) come here, now and then, and inquire about our little world, and when they find out it is so little that a streak of lightning can flash clear around it in the eighth of a second, they have to lean up against something to laugh. Then they screw a glass into their eye and go to examining us, as if we were a curious kind of foreign bug, or something of that sort. One of them asked me how long our day was; and when I told him it was twelve *hours long, as a general thing, he asked me if people where I was from considered it worthwhile to get up and wash for such a day as that.*

By this point in the book, Captain Stormfield's sense of self-importance is all but gone. The choirs of angels that sing as people walk in are annoying. He gave up trying to fly because you can think yourself to anywhere. He tossed his halo and harp aside (he never could play the harp well, and he wondered why he ever thought trying again was a good idea). He gave up all ideas that, even in Earth's heaven, he is special. This is a trend that continues to the end of the book, where he starts to enjoy life in Heaven for what it is. Having identified with Captain Stormfield, the reader goes through these changes as well. Sarcasm begins by being agreeable, and then becomes the ridiculous, at which point we agree that it's ridiculous.

The second way to embrace surreality and make it work for you is positively, loved for its absurdity, and not juxtaposed against anything. This is *surrealism*, which is similar to sarcasm, except there is no sense that you hate the surreality you weave. There's something about real life presented as absurd that's endearing, something about it that makes us love what we're being told. The passage I quoted from *Captain Stormfield's Visit to Heaven* isn't just sarcastic; you can see the love Twain has for the absurdity of the situation and how it opens our eyes. It makes us think of insects that only live a couple weeks, and wonder, "What's the point?" The oddness makes us love the idea of equating ourselves to an insect. It makes our eyes bug at our new surroundings. It tickles that self-loathing part of us that just wants to be humiliated and wronged. Reality feels enslavingly ordered and controlled.

Surreality is rebelliously wild and chaotic. We enjoy it the same way we enjoy being drunk (and there's even the hangover of coming back to reality, which is useful in itself as a rhetorical tool). But not everyone enjoys surrealism. In fact, it seems to be something that people either completely love or completely hate. If your opponent and audience love it, then you have your work cut out for you. Paint them a picture of wild, intentional, and abrasive inaccuracy. If your opponent likes it but your audience hates it, steer clear of surrealism. (None of this applies to sarcasm.) The same goes for when both your opponent and your audience hate surrealism. But if your opponent hates it and your audience loves it, by all means, piss off your opponent while gaining favor with your audience.

There's no right or wrong way to go about surrealism, but I have some tips for beginners. Start with a turn of phrase. Not a metaphor, but a figure of speech, an expression, an idiom, perhaps a cliché. Something like, "Plato was the bee's knees." Then set up the idiom as if you were speaking literally. "Plato was the bee's knees—weak, thin, and hardly worth mentioning. Of course, we do mention the bee's knees an awful lot, usually in an ironic way that makes them seem like a good thing to bring up. So I suppose when we bring up Plato, that's ironic too." Then go ahead and drag it out to the point where we forget what we were originally talking about, but be sure to bring it right back up at the end, as if you made a reasoned point. "Fortunately for the bee, the hive offers excellent medical benefits. But there is a hefty deductible, and treatment for arthritis of the knees, especially in knees as weak and thin and hardly worth mentioning as a bee's knees, is a long and astoundingly expensive process. The bee will need to take a second mortgage out on the comb, and work overtime to make payments. But he can't even do that because he's cooped up in therapy at the hospital and can't work, and falls so far into debt that the queen has to confiscate his comb. His wife is forced into hard labor and his children are sold into slavery, and the bee is still in debt up to his thorax. It's a sore subject for the bee. The whole situation is so terrible that I say don't bring up the bee's knees again. And don't bring up Plato either."

Let's try another, following the same formula. This is from a speech Kurt Vonnegut would have delivered at Clowes Hall in Indianapolis in April 2007, had he not died only days before. (You can find it in his posthumous collection of unpublished essays and short stories, Armageddon in Retrospect.) See if you can identify where each step takes place.

And somebody might now want to ask me,

"Can't you ever be serious?" The answer is, "No."

When I was born at Methodist Hospital on November eleventh, 1922, and this city back then was as racially segregated as professional basketball and football teams are today, the obstetrician spanked my little rear-end to start my respiration. But did I cry? No.

I said, "A funny thing happened on the way down the birth canal, Doc. A bum came up to me and said he hadn't had a bite for three days. So I bit him!"

But seriously, my fellow Hoosiers, there's good news and bad news tonight. This is the best of times and the worst of times. So what else is new?

The bad news is that the Martians have landed in Manhattan, and have checked in at the Waldorf-Astoria. The good news is that they only eat homeless people of all colors, and they pee gasoline.

That speech is chock-full of examples, as is Vonnegut's work in general. As a master of both surrealism and sarcasm, Vonnegut isn't so obvious about each of the steps I gave, but they are there. And he is able to work outside common figures of speech. With practice, you'll be able to do that too. In the meantime, the steps I gave will serve to give you a good feel for the possibilities while giving you a structure to work with.

So far, we've looked at two parts of argumentation: general fundaments and defensive tactics. These aren't exclusively fundamental or defensive of course, and all of it is applicable to offensive tactics, but generally if we haven't been talking of overarching things about language, rhetoric, and people, then we've been talking about how to back out of a corner. To recap, we discussed how language is instructional, how rhetoric is ubiquitous, what winning is, what the rules of argument are, and a few different types of audience and why it's important to remember them. We also discussed the need to gain control of vocabulary, the need to gain authority, the threat of boredom and how to fight against it, how to lie, how to sort-of lie, how to be surreal, and most importantly why you should let your opponent define your argument and how to do that while still appearing to be your own person. The last thing I'd like to talk about before going into the more offensive aspects of argument is delineation. And I mean *delineation* in two ways. First, I mean taking an argument off-course. Second, I mean showing that the argument is no longer linear, that it is complicated and multi-faceted.

Arguments are generally intended to go somewhere. To derail them is to stop them from reaching their destination. It's not that they couldn't make the point, it's that they got so far off-track there's no hope of getting to the goal in a timely manner. Notice the language I'm using here. *Derail*. *Off-track*. It's no accident that so many expressions about argumentation have to do with trains—though I wonder what people called it before the invention of the locomotive. Imagine that there are two engines on opposite ends of the train cars. This is a visual of an argument where you each bring your own arguments to the table. But since you are letting your opponent define your argument, there is only one engine. Your opponent is the engineer or conductor, and the audience members are the passengers along for the ride. You're a passenger too, but a rowdy one that's trying to crash the train. If you know anything about physics, you know you aren't going to topple the train over by pushing on the inside. It might strain the train, it might cause the train to shut down, but it will still be on-track and will resume its course after repairs. In an argument, you can do damage inside the line of reasoning by giving counter-evidence and such. But as soon as their evidence is repaired, the argument will move right along. Even if you got everyone else on the train, the audience, to push, any damage done will be to the train itself. Now, if you got everyone to rock back and forth and the train was going fast enough, it would derail—though it remains to be seen if the train derailed by the passengers or its own weight. Chances are the passengers helped, but the train was going to derail anyway.

To get the train to derail from the inside, you need to fuck with the engineer or conductor, because they control what the train does on the outside. Just to be clear if it wasn't already, to derail an argument is to take it off-topic and make it about something else. So all you really need is a good distraction. The distraction must be close enough to the original that nobody sees it for what it is—a different train on a different track—but sees it as the same train that has crashed.

This is where philosophy comes in. Philosophy

is, by its very nature, a derailment of language. I'll show you what I mean. Let's look at the most popular phrase in the history of philosophy: "I think, therefore I am." Start by asking where we find this phrase in ordinary, unphilosophical language. The reason we ask this is because no matter how much we think language is inoperable, everyday language gets the job done. And no matter how strict we wish language would be, everyday language works while being so unrefined. There's a definite sense in which we should hope our philosophical language is as good as our ordinary language.

We see bits of this phrase in our ordinary language: "I think I remembered to turn off the stove," "I think I'm going to throw up," "I think about her often," or in another form, "I thought so!" In each of these examples, *think* is a transitive verb. (It's a curious coincidence that it should be called *transitive*, with the root

Maybe that's

locomotives we

as far as I know,

the important part

how the subject inte

is definitely an intrar⋯⋯ ⋯ked

René Descartes, "Wh⋯ ⋯ou think?" he'd say, "It doesn't matter. What matters is that I do." So can we imagine a scenario where we would say "I think," intransitively? Two examples come to mind.

The first is in defense of oneself. I remember my dad once yelling at me for messing something up. He said, "Your problem is you don't think!" To which I responded, "I think!" So now, is the way that my dad and I used *think* the same as in, "I think therefore I am"? The difference I see is that mine was an objection, where Descartes' is not. My dad e literally no brain activity.

problem is you don't think things

which my response is therefore, "I think

through!" It's a transitive verb in disguise.

The second example is this: "What do you do when you lock yourself in that room?" "I think." Here, as with Descartes', it doesn't matter what I think, it's just what I do when I'm locked in that room. Is there a difference between this and Descartes' *think*? Yes, in that thinking-about-things (i.e. *thinking* as a transitive verb) is still the important part. *Thinking* itself is not what's accomplished by being locked in the room, it's thinking about things. With Descartes, the *thinking* itself is the important part because all he wants us to know is that he does.

What happens if we try to take Descartes', "I think," to ordinary language? I can only imagine an insane man on a sidewalk, shouting, "I think!" at passers-by. Someone might ask, "About what?" and the man would say, "Doesn't matter! Just, I think! Isn't that amazing?" What possible use could this, "I think," have? People would look at the man, confused, and that's about the time they'd come to the conclusion that the man is insane. (Then imagine that someone asked him to prove that he thinks. What do you think the man would say?)

Descartes invented a whole new sense of, "I think," that had never been used before. It was a private sense, one that could have no meaning to anyone else. Just as if I proposed that *grumfel* was the name of the color that I see when I see blue, and that *snozzits* was the name of the color you see when you see blue. How do we know they're different? How do we know what they are at all? How can these names possibly be useful to us? "The sky is very grumfel today." "Oh? I think it's snozzits."

You see, when I tell you, "I think about her often," it isn't at all necessary that you know what it is to think, in and of itself. As far as you know, *think* means "stare off into the distance with a furrowed brow." What *thinking* is doesn't matter. The only difference between Descartes' *think* and my *grumfel* is that *grumfel* isn't a word in any language at all, whether or not it has anything to do with the color blue. Descartes' *think* fools us because we use that word so often in ordinary language, in the ordinary way. And because it's written and said the same, even used in a somewhat relevant way, we think it has something to do with all the kinds of *think* we have in our ordinary language. But it doesn't. It has no more to do with "I think" in ordinary language than *grumfel* does with *blue*. Imagine if, instead of *grumfel* and *snozzits*, we said that the color I see when I look at blue is *periwinkle*, and the color you see when you look at blue is *navy*. I think we'd entertain the notion that we understand what it is I see in contrast to what it is you see for a bit longer. We could even start to reason it out—you tend to use adjectives that imply darkness when you describe the sky, and I tend to use adjectives that imply a light haze. Or something like that, and so on. But it's still a useless couple of words—they are, after all, the replacements for *grumfel* and *snozzits*. We just don't think of it that way, because we associate the ordinary uses of *periwinkle* and *navy* with *blue*, just as we associate Descartes' *think* with *think* in ordinary language.

And that's how Descartes derailed the debate about thinking. All of philosophy is language in an irrelevant and useless sense. But because it still bears the appearance of English, or whatever language someone might speak, we go right on thinking that we're still talking about the same thing that we were a moment ago. In other words, philosophy makes a perfect distraction for our train conductor. Suppose you're arguing with someone about whether or not a movie was good. They say it was good, and you say it wasn't. They bring up the acting, the writing, the direction, etc. as evidence that it was good, but you think all of those things are evidence that it wasn't good. Now, this is a matter of opinion, and there's no sure way to come to a conclusion that you both agree on because you think differently than each other. Believe it or not, most arguments are like this, but we argue them anyway because they're about topics we enjoy discussing, and so don't think that a matter of opinion can't or shouldn't be argued.

For a movie, what you can do is find some

despicable moral implication. If a story is any good at all, the characters will have flaws. Not one of them is respectable in every way (though if they are perfect characters, that's something you can bring up against the movie). Find one of those flaws in the protagonist, and make a big deal of it. Say that the movie promoted that flaw as if it is a good thing. Or in the antagonist, find something likeable and say that the movie is promoting bad people as if they are good. And then derail the argument by making the whole discussion about morality, rather than about the movie.

Or you can do the same for the story. Stories are a lot like arguments in themselves, in that they have a beginning, middle, and an end, they have a point, and so on. Any of the techniques I've already given to counter an argument can be used to counter a story. Particularly, you can find the hypocrisy of a story by finding at what expense it makes its point, and then how it needs what it expended. For example, you are talking about a movie that's a love story where two people work against incredible, extraordinary odds to love each other in peace. The story tells of this love at the expense of normal, everyday love, because normal, everyday love isn't good enough—extraordinary love is touching because of the struggle. Normal, everyday love by extension can't be touching like this, because it doesn't persevere by overcoming incredible, extraordinary odds—it perseveres by overcoming normal, ordinary odds. That's what makes it every day love.

Now we can take this criticism and recontextualize it from the movie to, in this case, problems of society. We can say that this is just one of many such movies that have led to a general unhappiness in society, where we have ordinary love but wish we had extraordinary love, because that's what we see in the movies. This movie is a symbol of all that has gone wrong with society, from the rise in divorce rates to the decline of small farm towns. Love stories like this are a kind of sensationalism that tells people not only to loathe what they have, but to have outrageous, impossible, and ultimately self-destructive ambitions. And anyone who doesn't have those expectations and instead found a comfortable, reasonable life flipping burgers and married to an ugly person is looked down upon, as if there's something wrong with *them*, as if the people disillusioned with Hollywood, the epicenter of illusion, are sick.

And so on. The state of society has nothing to do with the movie, but it sure sounds like it. Feminist groups do the same thing when pornography comes up in discussion. They say, "Porn subjugates women by giving men false expectations of what sex should be." What they don't say is they don't mean the women actually in the films. (Or maybe they do mean to include porn stars, but haven't thought about the fact that not only have they chosen to have sex on film, but doing something so personal in public requires a lot of guts—a lot of guts that someone who didn't *want* to wouldn't have done it. If porn stars are subjugated at all, they choose to be, and that's their right.) The issue of porn subjugating women has nothing to do with pornography itself. It's a derailment of discussions about pornography. It is philosophy. The reason they don't mention this is that when we think of women subjugated through porn, we think of the porn stars, which lends an immediate sense of victimization to their argument. Very persuasive stuff. And it's persuasiveness that we're after here.

When I've had discussions like this about movies where I derail the argument, they usually end with a pitiful, "Well, I like it." The *well* in that sentence is my claim to victory. *Well* is an admittance of everything I've argued. I don't need to change the "I like it" part. I just need them to admit I'm right. The same goes for the few times my opponent has a little more nerve and says, "You have your opinion and I have mine." That doesn't negate anything I said. It only minimizes what I said, or attempts to.

One of the rules in chess is, if your king isn't in check but it can't move, and you can't move any other pieces, the game is a draw. But this says nothing about what pieces I have left. Pieces are worth points. If I have more points, I win. The same goes for the situation of our argument about movies:

just because it's a stalemate doesn't mean I didn't win. I clearly did. Claiming an impasse is a defensive move that only means my opponent didn't lose clearly. They lost, and that's all there is to it. Anyone listening to the argument will lean my way, dazzled by how apparently complex my reasons are for disliking the movie compared to my opponent's reasons. And those are points that my opponent doesn't have.

That brings us to the second half of delineation: obfuscation,   or   the complication of things.   You can derail any   argument   by   throwing   some philosophy at it. But what happens when philosophy is thrown back at you? What happens   when   your   opponent   doesn't throw   their   hands   up   at   the   idea   of hurdling the mountain you placed before them   to   get   to   their   conclusion   on   the other   side?   You   need   a   bigger   tool. Derailing the train wasn't enough. You need to put down so many tracks that the train can't get down any of them. This is where many of the tools we've talked about come in handy. For example, if an opponent brings up any principles or ideologies, you can   explore   the   extreme   applications   of   those principles to find the exceptions. You might even be sarcastic while you do it. Or crack a joke. And meanwhile, show how hypocritical it is when it takes advantage of what it isn't. But these things won't take care of you all the time. Sometimes, instead of exploring the extremes to find the exceptions, explore the extremes to find complications. In these cases, completely discrediting their argument isn't the goal, but marginalizing it by discrediting their ability to think about the argument very thoroughly.

Let's go back to that love story movie, but reverse the roles so that we liked the movie and our opponent claimed that it was a symbol of everything wrong with society because it elevates extraordinary love above ordinary love. To delineate the argument, we must complicate the matter to minimize the damage done by their philosophical tirade. We might start with, "I agree that it's a truly sad fact of our society that people are unhappy with an ordinary life because they have unreasonable expectations. And I agree that love that prevails against all odds is no match for the ordinary love people take for granted. But like it or not, neither you nor me, nor that movie are responsible for the condition of our society. Furthermore, like it or not, you and I are both guilty of having unreasonable expectations—for example, you have unreasonable expectations of Hollywood. You think movies should do something profound instead of entertain. But believe me, trying to show a know-it-all like you something profound is like trying to show a blind person how big the sun is. It's difficult for *me* to comprehend and I can see the damned thing.

"On top of all that you're ignoring freedom. First, you're ignoring the freedom of each and every person to be as lawfully stupid as they like. Second, you're ignoring the freedom of the artists who made the movie to make whatever art they please. People should be free to express themselves. Now, I know you don't want to take away that right, but it confuses me why you don't mind that that's how you come off. It's like a not-racist person telling only racist jokes. I can understand having these completely (unreasonable) narcissistic desires in private, but in public? Shoving them down my throat as if you made any sensible point at all? It's good to be passionate about what you believe, and I applaud you for it, but perhaps you could find a way to do it without berating everyone that might care as well."

This rebuttal complicates the matter by making our opponent's argument an issue of rights, both of the audience and the artist, and is further complicated by what that argument tells us about our opponent themselves. If there is any sort of philosophical retort, you can do this again and again, just as academics in philosophy have done for over two-thousand years, until your opponent gives up. If the retort is non-philosophical, retreating back into ordinary language, either it will go back to the topic of the movie or it won't. If it's back to the movie, then you're either back where you started and you can do the whole thing again, or you're at that point where your opponent says, "It's a matter of opinion," and you win. If it's not back to the movie, then it's likely a reaction to something you accused them of, and they want to show that you're wrong by giving a real-life example. (This is what happens often when talking about homosexuals to a homophobe. They say, "I have plenty of gay friends," or something along those lines.) All you need to do is point out that it's irrelevant, because here they are, saying the things they're saying.

I used the issue of freedom to delineate in this

example, but my favorite and I think fail-safe issue to use is language itself. No matter how hard someone might try, they can't speak without using language. This makes every issue an issue of playing with words. Remember this argument and explore it as much and as often as you can:

There is nothing. If there is something, it cannot be known. If it can be known, it cannot be communicated.

This comes from Gorgias, Socrates' greatest opponent, a master of rhetoric. You can use this with absolutely anything, but let's switch roles with the movie again and respond to the accusation that we are impinging on freedoms.

"Freedom is just a word. It's not something people have because it's not anything. Or if it is something, it's not like we can know of it. Or if we can know of it, it's not like we can talk about it *without* using the word. It's a word at its very essence. And in this case, it's a word that you're using to guilt me into submission. Well, sticks and stones may break my bones, but words will never hurt me. You know what will hurt me? A society that can't offer enlightening entertainment because it's forgotten how to give it. And it's forgotten because it was too wrapped up in selling people silly dreams for too long, to the point where silly dreams were all people cared about, and so silly dreams were all that was produced. Words or no words, that's a world I loathe. And like a fish that's watching the ocean evaporate into a desert, I'm scrambling for any puddle I can find before it's all gone. You can call that narcissism all you want. Throwing words at me won't change the fear I feel. And until it seems hopeless, I'm going to fight for the preservation and increased demand of puddles. So in the interest of not only myself but of every fish out there, I say this movie fucking sucks."

Of course, my opponent could try to use the language issue to delineate as well, but if that happens, the result is two people recognizing that they're playing with words and the whole thing becomes a joke to them both. As the first to bring the issue of language into the picture, I count that as a win.

Let me end this chapter on a personal note: the greatest mistake of my argumentative life was publicly announcing that I was quitting philosophy. That was how I ended my book, <u>The Absurdity of Philosophy</u>. I meant that I would quit taking philosophy seriously, as anything *but* an obfuscation of the things I love. I didn't mean that I'd stop using it to delineate arguments. Now anyone that can't read well enjoys pointing out that I quit philosophy when

I'm clearly using it in order to discredit me and my argument. I would like to say to those people, once and for all: Yes, I quit philosophy. But I'm more than happy to use it against you.

As I've said before, argumentation and politics have a lot in common, so with this chapter I'm going to summarize Niccolò Machiavelli's <u>The Prince</u> in terms of argumentation by more or less interpreting political power as rhetorical authority, and the keeping of a country as the keeping of an audience.

Authority is either inherited or new. To inherit authority is to be seen as the spokesman for authorities people already subject themselves to. To have new authority is to have made your own by winning arguments without relying (explicitly) upon established authorities. It's easier to inherit authority than it is to make it. As long as you don't stray from the style and arenas of established authorities and are careful to remind people periodically of those established authorities, people will accept what you say without a fuss.

But when you make yourself an authority all your own, keeping people docile can be much more difficult; people will either treat you as they tend to treat authority—which is, submissively—or they won't because they're not used to having an authority around at all. There is nothing more difficult or unpredictable than establishing a new order of things. You'll always have enemies in those who benefitted from the old order, and flimsy supporters in those who think they might benefit in the new, as they too take on your enemies. Plus, people are generally only half-confident in things they haven't tried.

Immediately after winning an argument with the people who are accustomed to submission, be wary. In switching to you for something better, they've got a taste of what changing authorities can do for them, and they may make a habit of it. If you ever suspect you will need to defeat an argument or authority, do it immediately. The longer you wait, the more opportunity people have to explore their options and build up the nerve to challenge you. Plus, this makes people fearful of you, further establishing your authority. Having trounced problems immediately, you set a precedent for what happens to people, arguments, and authorities that might do the same. So take care of rebuttals early, because you can't avoid them, only postpone them—and the strongest rebuttals are bound to come first.

Those who aren't accustomed to authority are difficult to handle for obvious reasons—people don't put up a fuss if their customs are maintained, and submission is not one of their customs. You must either completely discredit or constantly supervise this kind of person until they become accustomed to submission. You could let them be autonomous but reliant on your authority after winning an argument with them, and that might work for a while, but they'll inevitably find a reason to revolt against you. For example, suppose you persuaded a crowd of punk rockers that Brittney Spears' music was actually pretty good. How long do you think that will last without the complete demolition of everything they believe? How long must you hang around to argue your point again whenever someone disagrees? I'd guess around two minutes, at which point you'll have either to kill them all or argue it again. Having said that, I should also say you must either praise or crush all arguments. Minor victories or remaining idle allows the same arguments to be brought up again. Major victories do not allow the argument to rise up again, because the audience will hold your opponent to their loss. That's the kind of progress you want.

Do not let authorities exist that could trump your argument. Do not try to align yourself with them. They will make your argument weaker by decentralizing your authority, and in turn make themselves stronger. Of the authorities you will face, they will either be centralized, putting you in situations where it's their word against yours, or decentralized, where authority of an argument is delegated to several other authorities. Centralized authority is very difficult to defeat in an argument, but if you can, it is much easier to maintain your authority afterward. For example, it's very difficult to win an argument where it's your word against your opponent's, but if you *can* win, your word will always win against theirs (or at least, if conflict arises again, you know how to defeat it). By contrast, decentralized arguments are very easy to defeat, but very difficult to maintain, since the delegates retain their authority. The reason is that you haven't defeated *those* authorities, only the argument that held them together and made use of them. Often, you will turn the delegated authorities against the whole of the argument, and that's how it will collapse. But that doesn't mean those authorities are loyal to you now. If your opponent is arguing for intelligent design, for example, they are probably drawing upon both scientific and religious sources. You can use both of these sources against your opponent to defeat them, but even when that happens, it does not mean they will submit to you. Those same scientific and religious sources could be used against you, since both you and your opponent, by using them to your own means, are placing them into contexts in which they were not exactly intended. Whether or not you can control these delegated authorities has nothing to do with you or how good you are—it is entirely up to the nature and character of those sources.

But, in general, winning arguments does depend on how good you are. Or, sometimes how lucky you are—but don't count on luck. Your abilities and the strength of your arguments will make opportunities for you. Luck will give you opportunities as well, and if you're lucky enough to be lucky, it would be a shame if you hadn't the abilities or a strong argument to take advantage of it.

Those just starting out will find that gaining rhetorical authority is very difficult, but once you start it gets easier. Making brand-new arguments is always difficult because people are used to the arguments they hear all the time, and will want to reject changes to the argumentative traditions of a topic. Most people want to see how well an argument works before they submit to it or use it themselves, so they will attack it to find the soft spots, the places where the argument is vulnerable, and exploit them. The question is whether you should rely on other authorities to succeed while starting out, or whether you can rely on your own abilities. The wiser choice is to rely on other authorities, because if you can't be stronger than them, at least you can do just as well. But if you don't practice going beyond those other authorities, the only authority you will ever have is theirs, which makes you inconsequential. And if you are inconsequential, then the audience will easily trade you for someone else, someone with more practice and originality. This is why starting out is so difficult: you must gain authority through others and surpass them. But once you get the hang of it, it's smooth sailing.

Now, there are those who gain authority through luck alone, or at least, not through a practiced talent for arguing, through chance or given authority by other people. Those who get authority through chance—the dumb luck that made them win an argument on accident—are not practiced and take no pride in their argumentative lives. They find it easy to win an argument, thinking only of those times where their luck prevailed. But they are just as likely to lose the next time as they are to win. It takes work to get your average above 1:1, work that will have you studying your opponents, practicing tactics, and building enough esteem to argue publicly. (It's only when you win an argument publicly that your authority strengthens faster than one person at a time.) Those given their authority by other people also might not be practiced, and thus are just as likely to lose as well, letting all their supporters down.

If you are practiced (or at least have a natural charisma and a knack for winning) and gained your authority through other people, you must be wary of those people, because while you rise higher and higher, they cling to you—but only for as long as they think they are doing better with you than against you. There *are* those who would build someone up just to break them down and better their own authority. And there is a very real sense in which you share your authority with the people that give it to you, and they will act like you owe them something. Not only does this division of authority weaken you, but it strengthens them like a giant, black, pulsing leech on the side of your face, taking all the credit for your good looks. (The leech is right you know, but this isn't about who is right. It's about you not having the balls or talent to stand up and take all the credit for

your good looks with a fucking leech on your face.)
You must act as if you deserved authority all along,
regardless of their instigation and support. But be
careful not to push them aside before building
enough authority on your own to carry you.
Prematurely piss off those people and they'll tear you
down faster than they raised you up, and make an
example of you to all those that might betray them.
The people that give you rhetorical authority must be
degraded so gradually that no one suspects you of
cruelty or trickery. While you can dominate people
into submission through cruelty, and you may get
them to behave as you wish, you'll never dominate
their minds, and they will conspire against you to
overturn your authority. (And dominance gained
through cruelty isn't exactly rhetorical authority
anyway, not in the sense we're using it now, because
they have no trust in cruel words. They fear you, not

your rhetoric. The difference between dominance and authority is the difference between submission and persuasion.) However, if you must be cruel to anyone, perhaps through insults or lies or bent truths, be quick about it. Not only does this take people by surprise, but it allows you to exert your authority mostly peacefully and well afterwards. It wears on people's nerves to be hurt repeatedly over time, and they'll rebel or at least shun you before you approach rhetorical authority. You can't rely on people that you degrade often, both for support and for authority—the latter because you've been destroying the authority you now ask them to give you again.

Regardless of how you may gain authority, make every effort to win the trust and affections of the audience or you'll have no hope in a losing situation (and you can't avoid losing, so get used to it). Whether you win or lose the argument, your rhetorical authority will hold if you have the audience's trust and affection. But don't be smitten with them in return. Maintain a healthy skepticism as to whether they trust you. You can never be too sure, and it keeps you on your toes to stay a step away. However, as long as you make them rely on you for their arguments and persuasions, they will not fail you, and you can trust them that far.

One certain measure of your rhetorical authority is whether you can make your argument alone, or if you must rely on other authorities, and if so, how many other authorities you need and how much you rely on them. Inside every human authority is a delicate ego. If yours is injured, you will lose your composure and likely your audience by that time. That ego is what needs protecting, and its delicacy is why you must take care in how your arguments and authority are supported. If you can field your own arguments, you need no help from anyone to maintain your ego. So long as you call upon the authority of others, your authority is indebted to them. And in relying upon other authorities, the best you can do is protect your ego by deflecting attacks to those authorities. Keep your audience happy and you won't have anything to worry about. Anyone who might argue against you will hesitate at the prospect, and because your audience is happy, you have no need to worry about them turning on you.

But it is best to provide your own authority and arguments. And you can't have one without the other. Whenever you bring on an authority, their argument will grow stronger, and at the expense of your authority. Or I suppose the authoritative person you hire, in a sense, might be completely incompetent and simply ruin you by association and by being an unreliable crutch for your argument. So while you can keep your ego in a jar of other authorities and maintain it pretty well, you can't really call your ego secure, because it is not your own jar. If I put a dollar in a friend's piggy bank for safety, guess who controls the dollar. No authority is weaker than an authority that doesn't belong to its user.

An authority ought to have no other aim or thought nor select anything else for study than argumentation and its rules and discipline, for this is the sole art that belongs to authority. Argumentation is so important that it not only maintains the authority of authorities, but allows new authorities to rise up from nothing, and established authorities to die. And authority is so important that, if you don't have it, people will simply not like you. Nobody likes *that* guy, the sniveling coward, always complaining to people that can't help him. Even when you're not arguing to build authority, you should be practicing. Every spat and difference of opinion is an opportunity to practice, and you should take it. In this way you prepare for arguments that determine a good deal of authority. And it's practice for not only winning, but more importantly losing, because knowing how to lose and still be thought of well by your audience is better than a talent for winning. That is, if you only know how to lose and not win, you can still build authority for yourself and trust from the audience. In this way, a losing argument can still be a good argument. But if you only know how to win and not how to lose, you will do more damage to your authority and ego in those fateful moments of loss.

And they are fateful. Some people envision a talent for winning so grand they never lose, and they think therefore that this is the ideal, but there is no such talent like that. How things *do* happen is so far removed from how things *ought* to happen that anyone who abandons what is done for what ought to be done will destroy themselves. It seems important to me that our methods reflect a healthy grasp on what accomplishes our goals, rather than what accomplishes ideals; important that we base our tactics on effectual truth rather than an imaginary one. Ideals are rules we make for and impress upon ourselves. There is no end to ideals, only continued slavery under them. Being good is a wonderful thing to people, and you're either very fortunate or simply talented if you can appear good. But goodness is not an ideal for us. If it serves us better to be a teeny bit wicked, or even downright evil, then that is what we should do. Good and evil are judgments of actions. No action is, by itself, good or evil. Holding an ideal of goodness can only lead to failure as you sacrifice your best argument for an apparent goodness in your actions. And it's not just goodness, but truthfulness, honesty, rationality, logic, godliness, professionalism, and on and on down the line of self-imposed handicaps. I know it's praiseworthy to have each of these things, but since it's impossible to have all of them completely, because the human condition does not permit it, it is necessary to know that these virtues are vices if sought, and to be prudent enough to know which of them would lose you your authority in a given situation, and which can be indulged with less concern.

Be careful not to be too generous with your authority, letting just anyone use it. The more people that use you, the weaker you become because you cannot keep up with every challenge to your authority their opponents might make. And you cannot control so many different presentations of your argument, which if looked at collectively will make you appear to be so many people. This happens all the time. Karl Marx, for example, saw the rise of "Marxism," and after seeing its tenants, commented that if that's what Marxism is, he, Karl Marx, was not a Marxist. Jesus Christ is another example, and though he didn't live to see it (as far as we know), the apostle Paul did. And who knows, maybe Paul was part of the problem. Either way, you do not want this same fate. Build large followings, yes, but do it slowly, so that each new generation of followers has time to adopt your methods in a near-imitative manner. At the very least, if your authority is stretched too thin, people will not respect you because you will appear to not defend your arguments.

Don't hesitate to be ruthless or cruel when arguing, if the situation calls for it. A few damaged egos will go far to keep audience members from becoming opponents. Kindness as a rule is praiseworthy, but it also shows weakness. It shows you are not willing or capable of standing up for yourself when attacked, and it will attract opponents. This may result in the audience not loving you, but they will fear you. And since fear is a far greater barrier for people than love, when you can't be both loved and feared, it's better to be feared. But make sure that their fear does not dissolve into hatred. Though people may fear you, if they hate you, their hatred will guide them to revolt against you and challenge you. In those kinds of arguments, your ruthlessness will be matched by theirs, and will not work. Maintain their trust, and you'll avoid being hated.

Everyone knows you should tell the truth, but notice that all major authorities have taken the truth and embellished some part of it in some way to the point of lying. If you're smart, you'll tell the truth when it benefits you, and lie when it benefits you. Bleeding hearts for honesty are forgotten soon enough, and you do not want to be forgotten. Yes, it's advantageous to appear honest, and you should do your best to appear honest, but you must be willing to bullshit if it's more beneficial. Everybody can see you, but no one knows how you really are. Deep down, they know as much, and they will judge you according to the outcome of a debate, not how honest you are.

Don't ever try to destroy the authority of someone who loves and trusts you. Their authority is yours, and you only weaken yourself. Similarly, don't destroy the authority of someone who relies on you completely. In a different sense, their authority is yours, and you are weakening yourself.

Nothing will advance your authority more quickly than taking on a large and perhaps seemingly impossible task. Convicts will tell you that on your first day in prison, either kick the shit out of the strongest guy in the room, or become someone's bitch. This is why. And it applies to argumentation: in a new situation, if you think you are capable, take on the most authoritative person around. If someone who loves and trusts you accomplishes something big, find a way to congratulate them, because you want to appear to appreciate the talent and practice that was required of them. It makes you seem like you've been there before. But if their accomplishment affects you negatively, bring them down. Never remain neutral on anything that affects you. If two people are arguing and the argument borders anything you argue, take a side. Whether or not your ally wins, they'll be grateful and feel indebted, placing you at the top of the hierarchy of authority because they will feel they could not have won without you. But avoid allying yourself with someone who could beat you in an argument, because if they win, you might be considered one of their followers, rather than the other way around.

Be picky about the people you keep close and confide in. People judge you by the people you keep close (or the lack of people, which conveys the notion that you cannot keep friends or that you have no allies, neither of which are enviable judgments). If you ever hit a rut for ideas, then you must be able to discern which of your friends' ideas are good and which are bad. But unless you are picky in choosing friends, you'll end up with nothing but ass-kissers. You must show that you aren't afraid of criticism, but you mustn't let just anyone criticize you, or people won't respect you because there are no boundaries that naturally come with authority. Pick smart friends, and only allow their criticisms, though only when you ask for them. Listen carefully to the criticisms, but make sure your decisions are for your own reasons. Be careful not to give your friends more authority than you have, or they'll try to take yours. People are just so squirmy, and they'll undermine your authority if you don't force them to submit.

If you follow this advice, your arguments will soon have all the authority your ego will ever need. But know that it's disgraceful to lose all your authority once it is established, and damned near impossible to regain. If you lose it, it's not bad luck, it's not anyone's fault but your own. Laziness brought about your downfall, because you didn't take heed and practice your art. It's disgraceful because your ego will be so shattered that you run and hide and hope for dear life that someone will resurrect you. You can only rely on defenses that you and you alone control, so it's better to be bold than timid, because luck be a lady that must be beaten into submission.

It is typical to characterize Niccolò Machiavelli as believing that the end justifies the means, and I'm sure it will also be typical to characterize the methods of argumentation I'm giving you similarly. I don't think of it that way. I do not think that the end justifies the means, and I think Machiavelli would agree with me. The idea behind "the end justifies the means" is that you justify doing something not good to accomplish something good. Again, there is no end to ideologies. We're trying to win, we're trying to gain rhetorical authority. Goodness doesn't enter into the matter. So the fact that we may do something morally or socially bad doesn't matter. We aren't trying to *justify* immorality. We're trying to win. Or, if you want, we could characterize winning as good, so that "the end justifies the means" is not a moral matter. In that case, every step Machiavelli and I gave is good. We aren't sacrificing authority in the hope that we win. We are gaining authority in the hope that we gain authority. The means justify themselves. The end justifies itself.

Now, perhaps you take moral issue with the methods that we give. That's fine. Don't use them. Nobody is asking you to do what you feel is wrong. My advice is that you give up arguing completely and live a life of moral goodness and be happy. These methods are not for you. These methods are for those who would rather gain authority and win than be moral. And as that is the case, I'll impress upon you to not enter back into the fray of immorality by judging us as immoral. Judgment is a matter of conviction, conviction is a matter of arguing, and argument is not possible without subjugation. The same goes for politics. Government requires some degree of oppression, or else nothing is governed. Politics are not for moral people, and there is no need to justify government's immorality, since all that needs justification is oppression, and the benefits of oppression are plenty. You are hindered, not helped, by your morals. You are the ruled, not the ruler—first by your morals, then by us. But that is why I won't try to talk you out of it: whether you argue or not, you're still subject to the debate as long as you show up to listen. We like you, people that are willing to lend us authority without discretion, without question, without a fight. That's the cost of consistent goodness. "Give unto Caesar what is Caesar's," wasn't just a smartass answer Jesus gave to religious leaders.

But back to "the end justifies the means." There are people who would have their means justified by the end. They typically subscribe to the ideal that they must stop at nothing to see it through, which is dangerous because while killing isn't something people normally get on board with, ideals are, and they'll drive people to the end of the world. For example, many socialists around World War I, II, and later tried to convince people that sometimes you must bite the hand that feeds if that hand is standing in your way of a world where nobody bites anybody's hands. You must kill people that stand in your way of a world where nobody kills each other, where everything is plentiful, and manna drops right out of the fucking sky. The difference between this and what Machiavelli was after when he said to kill dissenters as quickly as possible is that, as a prince, you shouldn't think killing dissenters is wrong. Wrongness doesn't enter into the matter. It must be done, so do it quickly. You must bite the hand that feeds if the hand is feeding you arsenic. With an ideal of socialism, they were willing to kill for a peaceful, utopian way of life. You *must* kill to overhaul a government, but to kill to have peace is just silly. Peace isn't even a guarantee. It's an ideal. The only time you need to kill someone in government is to reestablish authority, and authority, that inherently oppressive status, cannot bring peace, only order. And as the father of this order is death, no one should be surprised at the family resemblance. It was foolish for the socialist movements of that time to focus all their attention on the prize and swing blindly at whatever obstacle stood in their way. That is an example of trying to use the end to justify the means. Machiavelli's approach and mine are not.

 "Might makes right" is another proverb I'll be accused of professing but don't, because I don't believe in right or wrong. I believe that we as a society determine what is acceptable, yes, but might isn't always necessary to do that. I think right and wrong are attitudes individuals have about things, and even if might is used against an individual to make them say something is right, they may not actually agree. You can turn the thumbscrews on someone until they say the Catholic Church is right, but that doesn't mean they actually believe that. Likewise, while an entire audience may be pressuring you to submit, it doesn't mean that you will. So how is might making right? It doesn't. It makes an overwhelming pressure to submit. And submission is what you're after, not rightness.

Let me illuminate it this way: my wife and I are

arguing over the color a wall is painted. I say it's painted red, she says it's painted orange. Whoever wins is only *right* insofar as the other person submits. But the color of the paint doesn't change when the argument is over, only what is acceptable to call it. So right and wrong don't enter into the matter.

Now, one way we might solve the discrepancy is by calling in our roommate, Karen, to tell us what color she calls the wall. If she says it's red, then this puts a terrible pressure on my wife to submit. And likewise, if Karen says it's orange it puts pressure on me. But it's not as simple as that. If Karen says it's orange, then I might pull out an example of what I call orange to compare it to the wall. This also creates pressure, but there is no power of numbers here. It's just me and my color sample against two women who are probably menstruating. The menstruation also creates pressure, this time on me, because nobody wants to incur the wrath of bleeding women. And so on and so forth.

So yes, might often helps make things acceptable, but it's not the only means. And it still has nothing to do with right and wrong. The confusion over being right and being acceptable may still be a problem for you. Look at it this way: *right* has a sense of immutability to it, while *acceptable* has no such sense. The feeling that there is something wrong with "might makes right" is therefore very natural, since we understand might to be as whimsical as the people who make it, and that doesn't fit well with the word *right*. (Yes, this argument is over semantic choice, just like the color of the paint on the wall, but I'm not calling in any third party to convince you, thereby implicitly proving my point.) As I said, I don't believe in right and wrong. I don't believe in anything immutable. Even the laws of physics will eventually come to pass. Might certainly does not make immutable things. Might makes trends. And since trends are all we have, it's a good thing to have them on your side consistently if you want any rhetorical authority at all. That means having might behind you, supporting you, as well as other things that hold sway over trends.

Now, I will admit to saying that I am right. In fact, I say this often. I say it because immutability always seems stronger to us than trends, and so when I say it, I'm attempting to get a leg up in an argument. But people will only believe that, even if just a little bit, because I stay on top of trends. As long as I go with the flow while making it appear as if the flow is mine, I am continuously on the acceptable side of things, and so appear right. It's an essential ingredient of authority.

It can be hard for people, seasoned debaters or not, to avoid looking shallow while summarizing their opponent's argument. This is essentially a side effect of summarizing itself, which requires simplification, and it's such a fine line between acceptable simplification and over-simplification that there is, in fact, no line at all. To avoid this embarrassment, I developed a tool in <u>The Absurdity of Philosophy</u> called *contrastruction*. The idea is that you take an argument you disagree with, and make it agreeable. Don't do this by changing the text, but by changing the sense of the text, or by changing its context. There is always a bit of ambiguity in the sense of a word so that, if you look the word up in a dictionary, more than one of its senses is applicable.

Context is that unsaid part of the words we say that helps us make sense of things. The more unclear the context, the more senses a word can have. For example, "I beat my wife." When I say that, it could mean that I injure her, or it could mean that we played a game and I won. If I say, "I beat my wife at chess," it's a little harder to interpret that as an admittance of violence against her. But it is still possible. (In this example, all we have are the words—if this was a real-life situation, the environment and the speaker become part of the context.) If *chess* is short for "chess club," then *beat* can still be interpreted as violence or winning, though with a little bit more weight on the winning side, since it's a place known for where games are played. Context is never perfectly clear for any words, so there is always room for reinterpretation. In order to contrastruct an argument you disagree with or don't like, you must reinterpret it so that you agree with the argument, and your reinterpretation is wholly consistent with the original. (That is, the words and known context haven't changed, only the ambiguous parts.) Like anything, contrastruction takes practice, and perhaps a little more than other argumentative tactics, because you'll need to have all this worked out in a fraction of a moment not to miss a beat. With this much of contrastruction, you should be able to avoid any unnecessary arguments, which will help maintain your posture as a person who doesn't simply argue to argue. You will be a person who only fights when there is something to fight. People could avoid so many arguments if they could recognize when they don't disagree, but simply have a different semantic selection for a topic.

However, that will only take you so far. Sometimes, even though you fully understand an argument because you understand its possible senses, you might still disagree with it. In those cases, contrastruction leads you to the values your opponent holds dear, because these values act like a beacon to align their argument and the context of the argument. These values are not reasoned, they simply *are*, and often cannot be communicated. They are unreasoned because they cannot be communicated—reasoning is done through communication, even if with oneself. If there was reasoning behind them, they wouldn't be seminal, and you'd be able to contrastruct them. These core values, these seminal points, are the weakest and the strongest part of an argument. They are the weakest because they are reasonless and wordless, and therefore confusing—all characteristics someone like me drools over. Like a dog on a leash just out of reach of a big fat steak, I wait my turn to speak to pounce. But are we men or are we beasts? We are men, and that means we can restrain ourselves a little better and think the situation through. These core values are also the strongest part of an argument, meaning that it will be almost impossible to change your opponent's mind about them. Furthermore, it will be nearly impossible to get your opponent to feel any shame for their lack of reason. You probably won't get them to feel any shame for not feeling shame either, because the audience and "everybody else" are likely to hold similar core values. We're all human after all. Anyone you're likely to argue against probably comes from the same culture as the audience and "everybody else." People tend to not be original at all, including you and me. Nobody is good enough to rely on changing people's core values. It doesn't matter how right you are: if you don't want an angry mob chasing you with a noose, you won't press the issue and you'll let their core values be. It's not your big fat steak.

So what do we do now? First, decide if this is somebody you will interact with much beyond this argument. This will let you know if you can make the destruction of their core values a long-term project. If not, then stick to the ambiguities to give yourself something to argue against that you understand. But if the relationship will last a long while, then you have time to recondition that person to dismiss those core values. They learned them that way, and they can be broken that way. Be supportive of those core values publicly (which will eventually make you their confidant) while implicitly undermining them with your advice and future discussions. Eventually their new convictions will be so strong that you couldn't keep them in their old ways if you tried. I've done this a number of times, specifically with Christians. I will side with a Christian against someone after contrastructing the Christian's argument. I argue against their opponent using the interpretation that makes the most sense to me. The Christian agrees, as anyone would who is getting argumentative help, and over time they adopt those arguments for themselves. The thing is, those arguments are founded on different core values—*my* core values. And sometime soon thereafter, they give up their Christianity, or at least whatever point of view it was they were defending. It's slow sabotage, but it works.

Either way, whether you plan on a long-term interaction with your opponent or not, your next step is to change your tone from forceful, headstrong, or whatever it is, to curiosity and compassion. You are going to attack from the ambiguities, and they will accept better any questions you ask or arguments you pose if it doesn't feel like you're dubiously trying to back them into a corner. Say things like, "I don't get why..." and "I'm kinda stupid with stuff like this, so can you walk me through it like I'm five?" Put on your best confused-but-curious face and let them think they know more than you. People respond well to this, thinking they're in a position of authority. It also gets you a simplified version of their argument, rather than creating it yourself and getting called on a misrepresentation. Then wait for them to hang themselves. As long as you direct them to those points of ambiguity and stay one step ahead of them in contrastruction, they'll contradict themselves or say something stupid. Then you'll pounce on it, at first with that confused-but-curious demeanor, but growing into authority and domination. People can't last forever, explaining away ambiguities. You see, an opponent proposing an argument is like someone telling you that they're really strong. Instead of challenging them with your own strength, be the fat kid that demands a piggyback ride. They won't last with you on their shoulders. Contrastruction, when it doesn't leave you agreeing with them, lets you know which way to lean and where to put dead weight.

But as they grow weary of supporting their argument, they'll grow weary of you. So you'll need to offer them alternatives to reinvigorate them and give them freedom from your harassment. Your alternatives should be a contrastruction for your opponent, remaining consistent with the words of their argument while contextually supporting your opposing position. If it's not—that is, if your alternative is quite clearly your opposing position with a message to abandon their argument—you will reinvigorate your opponent, but they will reject your solution. And so the argument continues.

(Remember, when you go head-to-head with someone, it's your word against theirs. To gain any ground, you must sacrifice some authority in order to create a disturbance large enough to take advantage of the ripples and come out ahead.)

So the goal is, whether over a long period of time or within the bounds of a single argument, to lead your opponent to your conclusion through their own contrastruction (because they're likely to not know how to do that) by taking advantage of the ambiguities in *your* argument that make it acceptable to your opponent. Doing this quickly enough to persuade your opponent during the argument is very, very difficult and will require mastery of the technique on your part. Anyone with a modicum of practice under their belt should be able to accomplish a victory with the long-term approach.

Even with contrastruction, there will be times when you want to attack someone for an argument they didn't make. This is called a strawman. The details of why it's called a strawman are still unclear to me. Some say it's like setting up a dummy to attack, instead of your opponent. Others say it's like a voodoo doll, where you attack the doll to attack your opponent by proxy. Still others say you must be really stupid to mischaracterize an argument, so you're like the scarecrow from <u>The Wizard of Oz</u>, wishing he had a brain. At any rate, you can be sure that the less your characterization of an argument looks like the real argument, the less acceptable it will be to your opponent and to your audience. And, I'll add, that is why people who think a strawman is named after the brainless scarecrow are right: an obvious mischaracterization will make you look stupid, whether you meant to do it or not. That doesn't mean don't do it—please do. Just be sure to hide it as well as you can.

I don't buy into the hatred of strawman arguments. As far as I see it, if someone says something incorrectly, you simply correct them and move on. By calling it a strawman, they make a big deal of it, as if the mischaracterization was intentional, or something someone does often. When I was a little boy, I asked my mom to buy me some candy while we were at the grocery store. She said, "We'll see, but I need you to be good while I'm shopping." So I was very, very good. Yet when it came time to check out, there was no candy. I asked, "Are we going to get some candy now?"

"No, not this time."

"But you said if I was good I could get some candy!"

There are a number of ways my mom could have responded, but it's interesting to note that she did not say, "That's a strawman. I said if you're good we will see, not if you're good we *will*." In fact, there was no reference to my mischaracterization of her words aside from what is necessary to correct me. "No, I said we'll see. We don't have the money right now." Why should it be any different for more robust arguments? The only difference is that calling a counterargument a strawman makes us think extra poorly of the guilty party.

The exact references behind a person's words are entirely inaccessible to us. Language is not a referencing system; it's a tool for utilizing each other. It is instructions. Even if language was a system of reference, nobody can know the exact reference anyone makes because we can't know what's going on in their minds. (It's in light of this that we know language can't be a system of reference, because it couldn't arise as one in any natural way.) *Every* time someone's argument is summarized or restated, it's a strawman. No way around that. So I ask again: why does anyone say that it's a strawman? It's redundant to say so, since it's a given. The answer is they want to make us think poorly of the person making the strawman. Considering the possibility that you didn't understand them and that's why you made a strawman, it's up to them to make themselves understood as they share the blame of your misunderstanding, and should therefore share in the negative thoughts they've brought upon you.

There is one last thing to consider about the legitimacy of calling an argument a strawman, and that's the possibility that we're only supposed to call,

"Strawman!" when we think the person is doing it intentionally. My response is: Prove it. We've already established that we can't know what's going on inside anyone else's mind. Proving it is impossible. Plus, if you knew they were doing it intentionally, why are you arguing with that person? You obviously chose your opponent very poorly, since they're willing to go places you are not, do things and commit crimes that you are not. You're in a losing battle, which is something you should have known beforehand, and if you couldn't know, you definitely shouldn't continue because now you know they don't care about winning by your rules. But you don't know they did it intentionally, you're still at square one, and if someone didn't understand, you share the fault.

Remember this argument in the event that someone tries to call a strawman on you. On the other hand, if someone mischaracterizes your argument in a way that you can explain well, take every advantage of the situation and decry the strawman. Be careful, however, because you may be called on your hypocrisy if you use the argument against calling strawman, and then call a strawman yourself. You won't succeed within a single argument, and you probably won't do to well in general either, across arguments, where the same people are watching.

But you don't need to call your opponent on a strawman to make the audience think poorly of them for it. As an alternative to calling someone on their strawman, simply walk them through your argument and demonstrate how it doesn't line up with what they presented. Take advantage of any discrepancy to show that you didn't say what your opponent says you said. This is what you'd be forced to do if you accused someone of making a strawman anyway, minus the redundancy of actually saying it. Your audience isn't stupid. They'll get it. And they'll think poorly of your opponent one way or another, whether they call it a strawman themselves or because your opponent comes off as slightly stupid for not paying attention. You can do this while defending yourself against any accusations of strawman simply because you didn't call a strawman while your opponent did, even though you were both guilty of the same thing. This tactic controls the vocabulary of the argument (which we've talked about already and is very important to winning) by making the word *strawman* give us a bad taste in our mouths. We are saying that it's okay to make a strawman as long as we don't call it that, which is difficult for anyone not practiced in argumentation beyond what you find in books about arguing.

There are actually many problems with the approaches in such books, like Clear Thinking: A Practical Introduction, by Hy Ruchlis, or Being Logical: A Guide to Good Thinking, by D. Q. McInerny. These books, and others with no regard for twentieth century rhetorical theory in general, teach readers how things *should* be and what people *should* do, rather than what actually works or what we actually do. When I first read Chaim Perelman's The New Rhetoric and I came across the chapter *Fact & Truth*, what I read was an account of the words *fact* and *truth* and when and how it's used. I did not read "This is how Truth should be, but often isn't for some people." I read, "This is how people use the word *truth* in English, and that's the only thing you can count on for any consistency when it comes to matters about truth." I did not read, "This is what makes something true," but "This is when people call something true." Idealistic books on argumentation are a complete waste of time. But they do leave us with some headstrong opponents who make themselves vulnerable. So we'll take a look at some more of these "rules of logic" to be prepared.

 *Logic* is a word that should be said less often. Yet I hear it all the time. "That's not logical." "Logic tells us to do this." And so on. We use the word the way a police officer uses *law*, except there are no logic police, and you might actually get in trouble for disobeying the law. Even if you could designate yourself as the logic police using an enormous amount of authority (which is all placed on the line for this policing, and you'll lose it if you don't police well), you don't get a blue uniform and badge. Or if you do—well, you're just a nerd. And just in case you are a nerd, I'll put it like this: it's the Romulans that should live long and prosper. Any ol' machine can be logical. There's something organic about nonsense. Try getting a machine to be illogical. It might be able to, but it'll be illogical logically.

Logic itself has no starting point. It does not begin. It is only applied to what's already there. It says nothing specific, only what you can say after you've already said something. What I mean is, if you know *what* makes an argument true, then and only then can you determine if something *is* true. Of course, truth is just a warm, fuzzy feeling we get about information that persuades us. And since you're in the middle of an argument, you're hardly in a position to say what does and does not persuade. So saying that something is or is not logical is a cheap rhetorical tactic to get people to think they already agree with you. Some of you are thinking, "I've heard people call things illogical in an argument before, and it didn't persuade me." That's precisely the point. It doesn't work. It's cheap because the very few people that it *does* work on only buy into it because the word *logic* is used. It must sound cool to them. It's certainly not because they know what logic is. Ask any one of them to show you something elementary, like a proof utilizing De Morgan's rule in prepositional notation, and they'll give you a blank look, which is nothing like a blank check—believe me, I've tried to cash a blank look at the bank. It's worthless, and therefore very cheap. And I don't use *logic* anyway just to build up a small crowd of followers to get the ball rolling. They're idiots and I can't rely on them to support me the way I want to be supported.

Logic is a game college people play with certain kinds of sentences. It's nothing more than that. It's not applicable everywhere, only to sentences, as it usually deals with the maintenance of truth, and only sentences can be true or false. The law of non-contradiction and the law of excluded middle are laws of logic, not laws of physics or laws in a legal system. So when some of you logic zombies insist that God is or is not logical, you're not just cheap, you're wrong. You're misusing *logic*. You might as well run up to the nearest Catholic bishop and call him a cheater for not walking diagonally, as the rules of chess mandate.

And speaking of the laws of logic, they're not set in stone. Not all logics demand that contradictions are false. Not all logics demand that something is necessarily itself. Not all logics demand that a double negative is a positive. And so on. We pick and choose the rules of logic depending on the sort of game we want to play. But unlike chess, the rules we choose aren't necessarily the same rules our opponents play by. Understanding that and arguing accordingly will save you a lot of embarrassment with failed presumptions and will go far to make you seem like a more thoughtful person.

Of course, if you're allowing your opponent to define your position and contrastructing everywhere else, you won't have the opportunity to call something illogical. But if you can't play by someone else's rules to see where they must be broken, then at least have the balls to play by your own rules, not the rules of stuffy old men who don't know a lick about language. Oh yes, make no mistake: logic, even the proper academic kind, completely misses the mark as any kind of formalization of language. I'll give you an example. "The sandwich was four months old, but I ate it anyway." We'll let *S* stand for "The sandwich was four months old," and we'll make *A* stand for "I ate it anyway." When formalizing that sentence into logic, how do you handle the word *but*? Turn it into *and*. That's right, according to logic, *but* and *and* are the same thing. So it's *S & A*, which literally means, "The sandwich was four months old and I ate it anyway." If you think about it this way, *but* and *and* really are the same thing. That is, if you ignore how *but* has the nuance of negation—"I ate the sandwich *despite* the fact that it was four months old." If you ignore irony and surprise and implication and context and nuance—then yeah, *but* and *and* are the same thing. Logic is nothing but this sort of gross overgeneralization. It's the nature of logic to oversimplify language—the degree of formalization demands that we ignore some things.

I'll give you another example. Think about when people actually use double negatives in their day-to-day lives. You might find a sentence like, "It's *not* that I *don't* like her, I just hate her." Logic's rules about double-negations would have us translate that sentence to "It's that I do like her, I just hate her." Or if we want it to make any sense at all, we can reword it to, "I like her, I just hate her." All nuance is lost. All sarcasm is bastardized and mangled. That is not the same sentence, it doesn't mean the same thing, and no logic zombie can argue otherwise without employing the same sort of tunnel-vision that logic used to come up with it in the first place.

So it comes down to this: You don't have the authority to police people's logic. Even if you did, you're not dealing with actual logic, just a word that apparently stands for whatever makes sense. And if you are dealing with real logic, you're assuming it does more than guide you through whatever you're assuming is true. If you're doing actual logic, you're not doing anything practical because logic forces you to oversimplify and outright ignore what's actually going on when we speak. It's a game. Not a badge, not some compelling ethereal force, just a game. Remember this the next time someone tries to force your hand with the dubious magical powers of logic.

A traditional law of logic that deserves its own chapter is that of identity. "A thing is itself." "*A* is *A*." Don't you believe a word of it. I'm going to give you a little bit of philosophy, but rest assured, it's not to delineate you, just the people you'll encounter that insist you use laws like the law of identity, to help you delineate them.

Think of a person's name in a sentence. "Joe is a plumber." Joe, the subject, is a single identity here, and the object is an aspect of Joe—he is a plumber. And *plumber* isn't what Joe is, but it's a sort of secondary name that helps us know what to do with Joe—contact Joe when you need a plumber. Now think of Joe in terms of the law of identity: Joe is Joe. That doesn't help us know what to do with Joe at all, it's just Joe's name repeated. And keeping in mind that language is instruction, since that sentence gives us no clue as to how to use Joe, it has no useful instruction. It is, in a word, meaningless. We can't know how to use it. It's like if we asked someone how to play chess and they told us, "A pawn moves like a pawn." We still know nothing. This is a law of logic. "A thing is itself." And logic is a game, like chess, yet you'll never find a rulebook for chess that will say, "A pawn moves like a pawn." No, a rulebook will tell you that a pawn moves forward one square at a time, unless it's the pawn's first time moving, when it can move two squares forward; pawns capture other pieces forward diagonally; pawns cannot skip a square occupied by another piece; and when a pawn reaches the opponent's end of the board, it may be traded for a bishop, knight, rook, or queen. *Now* you know how a pawn moves. The law of identity is useless because it gives no new information. It is not a rule that we can follow, because it has no instruction. (It is quite like Descartes' "I think" in that regard. It is no coincidence that the law of identity was formulated by a philosopher.)

But there are still people that insist you follow the law of identity, as if you *could*. There's no outright way of saying why they're wrong, so start by pretending they're right. Think back to Joe the plumber. *Plumber* is an aspect of Joe, a secondary name, but not the whole of Joe. We assume there's an automatic disconnect between *Joe* and *plumber*, or else there'd be no reason to try to relate them in a sentence—the sentence would be useless otherwise. The way we are told to understand "Joe is Joe" by the law of identity is that there is no disconnect. However, as I just pointed out, without disconnect, trying to relate Joe to Joe in a sentence is meaningless. It has no use. So since we are assuming the logic zombies are right that the law of identity is something we can follow, we must also assume that, like *plumber*, *Joe* is an aspect of Joe, a secondary name, but not the whole of Joe. A clear violation of the law of identity, because a thing is itself. *A* is *A*. Therefore, in order to *follow* the law of identity—something we can only do if there is disconnect between subject and object—we must break the law of identity.

Seeing as that's the case, I'll give you something useful about identity. Identity is the calling card of authority. It is the bell to the dog's slobber. Like authority, if you associate it with something else, that something else starts to inherit that identity. For example, to this day I can't hear the names of my parents on others without thinking about my parents. They're not the same people;

they have nothing in common except that they share a first name. The same goes for Elvis. I can't hear the name Elvis without thinking Elvis Presley. There are less extreme versions of this, such as my friend Tim, who likes Elvis Presley, and who people call "that Elvis guy."

As identity transfers, so does authority. Tim could just as easily be a fan of Richard Dawkins and be "that Richard Dawkins guy." Everything Tim says about matters that Richard Dawkins talks about will be regarded, by and large, with nearly the same authority Richard Dawkins himself has when he speaks about them. This extends to group identity as well, even to the proverbial "everybody else." It is possible to obtain the identity of your entire audience by simply associating yourself with them. The more you do it, the more everyone will believe it. It helps of course if they don't seem to disagree. To associate two identities, you need only place them in the same context, as part of the discussion, either implicitly or explicitly. However, there are complications with both approaches.

First, when you associate two identities implicitly, you run the risk of the audience not making the connection. And without the connection, there is no transfer of identity or authority. But if you make the association too obvious—unless you're telling a joke—you run the risk of appearing uncertain if it is a positive association, or passive-aggressive if it is a negative association. Passive-aggressiveness is a defensive—and usually losing—disposition. We'll talk more about negative association next chapter. You must recognizably imply the association in a way that leaves people feeling they alone "get it," or you will seem suspicious. To associate them implicitly, say the name of one identity in conjunction with characteristics of the second. Use indirect characteristics. For example, if you're implicitly associating George W. Bush with Adolf Hitler, it is not effective to call President Bush a Nazi. *Nazi* is too direct. You might try, "President Bush is a dictator who will stop at nothing to purge society of evil as he sees it." If we're led to think of who else shares these characteristics, Hitler is certainly the first person to come to mind.

Unless you are very talented, you won't be able to associate implicitly two identities by connecting the first identity's characteristics with the second's characteristics, without any names. It's too vague. And part of the problem with it as a whole is that you will often need to rearrange the order in which you give characteristics. What I mean is, Johnny Depp is an actor who plays music as well. Elvis Presley was a musician who acted as well. Anyone trying to compare these two men will have a difficult time of it, because you need to rearrange the order of one man's characteristics. "Johnny Depp is a musician who acts as well," or "Elvis Presley was an actor who played music as well." It won't convince anybody, even though both descriptions of either man are perfectly true.

Lastly, you should know that implicit associations are a good way to send out feelers and see if the audience will allow an explicit association or not.

When you associate two identities explicitly, you run the risk of oversimplification that is obvious to your audience. If this happens, your opponent can (and should) characterize you as someone who can't be trusted because you're hasty. That would be detrimental to any authority you have, so don't do it. Don't, as one young woman did, hold a picture of

President Obama with a Hitler mustache and ask Senator Barney Frank, "Why are you supporting a Nazi policy, as Obama has expressly supported this policy? Why are you supporting it?" Barney Frank's response was appropriate: "... It is a tribute to the first amendment that this kind of bio-contemptible nonsense is so freely propagated. Ma'am, trying to have a conversation with you is like trying to argue with a dining room table. I have no interest in doing it."

It's interesting to note in that example that, prior to what I quoted, he chided the woman for making such an absurd association between Obama and Hitler, but then went on to make an absurd association of his own, of this woman to a dining room table. Nobody criticized him for that. And that's the lesson to be learned about explicit associations: they're all right as long as most of the audience agrees. This applies to both negative and positive identity associations. Don't be hasty, send out feelers in implicit comparisons, and make explicit comparisons only if you think the audience will like it.

And by now, some of you are thinking, "That we can associate identities doesn't negate the law of identity. We don't confuse the Elvis guy with Elvis Presley himself." It's only a matter of degree. Pythagoras, for whom the Pythagorean Theorem is named, is credited with plenty of things he didn't actually do, such as the Pythagorean Theorem. His followers and even people that had nothing to do with him did that work. Yet, he is Pythagoras, the great Greek mathematician who developed the Pythagorean Theorem.

Another example ironically comes from Ayn Rand, who thought the law of identity was the first law of logic, and cited Aristotle as her inspiration for thinking that. Of course, if she had read Aristotle, she would know he thought the law of non-contradiction was the first law of logic. Nevertheless, tens of thousands of people who swear by Rand's writings know Aristotle as that guy who thought the law of identity was the first law of logic.

For more contemporary examples, ask yourself how many terrorist attacks are attributed to Osama Bin Laden, even though he had nothing to do with them. Don't think just of news outlets. Think of what normal people believe. Or ask how many things went wrong during the Bush administration are credited directly to President Bush. Or how many outrageous stunts by various rock stars are attributed to Ozzy Osbourne or Marilyn Manson? These aren't simply "that Elvis guy" associations. These are downright "that is Elvis Presley" associations. Or there's the matter of when someone is mischaracterized.   Did Michael Jackson just love children, or was he a pedophile?   There's hardly anyone that thinks he just loved children, yet that may just be the case.   The truth doesn't matter. Michael Jackson's identity is wrapped up in how people see him, not in how he saw himself, and not in how he actually was. The same goes for all of us, and anything we can identify, because identity isn't solid. Identity is as trendy and whimsical as clothing fashions. It is certainly not a law to found logic, and certainly subject to rhetoric.

Arguments are implied insults. Some arguments are obvious or even explicit insults, yes, but not all. But all arguments, including the most innocent disagreement in the most congenial conversation, are implied insults. You are not wrong in an argument, because arguments are against *opponents*, not reality. You are instead more ignorant, less informed, less perceptive, and not as good as your opponent. This is what your opponent is saying. Arguments happen the same, whether one person is right or neither. So again, arguments aren't about truth. They aren't about right and wrong or who is correct and incorrect. Arguments are about tearing down the other guy. And if you don't tear down the other guy, then you are torn down. This is, again, implicit. It begins with an explicit attack on something you believe or agree with or on vocabulary you condone. These things are the pillars you've built your authority around, no matter if they are very important pillars or not, so an attack on these things is an attack on your authority. This is where it became an implicit attack on you, because of the relationship between your authority and your identity, or ego. The only time you *might* be wrong is when you dissuade yourself of some belief you held. Even then, your new self, marked by your new beliefs, is insulting the person you used to be.

This book is called <u>You're Stupid</u> because that's all anyone says in an argument, in all the various meanings of that phrase, at least. In some arguments, you're stupid might mean you're intellectually slow, or you have yet to catch up. It might mean you tend to make poor decisions or conclusions, which must be true to be *wrong*. Or it could mean you are foolish or careless. Or your head is up in the clouds instead of "down here, where it belongs." Or the things you say or do are pointless, meaningless, or worthless. Anyone who argues anything believes at least one of these things about their opponent. If not, there cannot be an argument of any kind, from the most trivial childhood quibble to the most robust mathematical debate. It is the feeling that someone is stupid that motivates us to argue. Sure, you might not put it in those words, but then, before it was put into any words, it was implicit. "You're stupid" are simply the words I chose and I think they lead us to an interesting discussion we wouldn't have if other words were chosen.

Like any other time someone insults you, you must decide whether or not to defend yourself. If there's an audience, you must consider which of you has more credibility with them. You won't necessarily want to waste your time with an opponent if you have the audience on your side from the start. You can ignore this advice if the audience is thirsty for blood. However, if you don't think you can beat them—and be honest with yourself here—then ignore them even if the audience wants them to fall hard. Anything less than the total obliteration of your opponent and you'll lose credibility and authority for no reason at all. In cases where your opponent has enough credibility or authority to threaten your own, you must argue. In cases where you have less authority than your opponent, but not enough to pose a threat, you should argue. You have nothing to lose. This system of judging whether you should argue also applies to when you are considering insulting someone by starting an argument.

Another aspect of this is that we define who we are through conflict. Sure, we may have some rudimentary feeling of identity prior to putting it to words, but without words, there is no definition. Argument forces us to define ourselves. Insults force us to define ourselves. When considering whether or not to engage someone in an argument, you must first decide what sort of threat they pose to your identity, and think about how much work you're willing to put into defining and establishing your identity.

Academia characterizes insults as inappropriate for arguments. It was called an "ad hominem fallacy" to insult someone in order to win an argument. Think of facts as strings, dangling in the air.

A person who argues is like a pair of fingers

that pinch those strings together.

When someone makes an argument, they bring facts together. Your goal, as the opponent, is to pull the facts apart so they don't work together. And you have two options for doing this:

1) Pull the strings from out of the fingers, one by one.

2) Smash the fingers.

To come away from the metaphor, you can either remove the facts through a tedious process of either discrediting them or showing them to be irrelevant, of which most of this book details, or you can discredit the person by insulting them so that it doesn't matter what facts they use or how correct they may be. Insulting the person is not only easier, but it has a resonating effect on the audience. If they side with you, they will probably never give your opponent any credit, who will therefore probably never need to be debated again. That's a win you can count on. Whoever came up with "ad hominem fallacy" probably got called a pussy a lot for not being able to man up against someone calling him names. He just threw his hands up in the air and insisted that you can't do that. I don't know why people listened to him. If he could argue that insults distract arguments because they're completely irrelevant and therefore a dishonest means of winning an argument, he should have had no problem fighting against insults in the first place. But alas, the bells of history chimed to the turn of the hour, and it's now popular to call insults a fallacy. I say that insults are necessary to arguments, and therefore necessary for identity. It hurts but it helps, even though people might not like you for it. Of course, let's not fool ourselves: You don't insult people to help them. They are helped only if they can overcome the insult. You are insulting them to damage their identity, and that's the only excuse you need.

And it's with that in mind that you should consider whether or not to insult someone explicitly, whether or not to actually call someone or their ideas stupid. If you insult people too often, it's your insults and not your reasoning that your authority is founded on. And while that may work to maintain your authority with a single, long-term audience, it doesn't work well with new audiences because insults are generally frowned upon. So take care not to let audiences think that insulting people is all you can do. (I suppose that applies to the implicit insults in arguments as well; take care not to let audiences think that arguing is all you can do.)

But if you have to be so careful with explicit insults, should you simply not make them? Despite what you may think, it is rare that you'll engage an argument where you shouldn't explicitly insult *someone*. There are three cases where you shouldn't:

1) When you and your opponent are alone. Explicit insults are for the benefit of your audience. Insults summarize succinctly that you disagree with your opponent, or even despise your opponent or their ideas. They give your audience a sort of anthem to stand behind. The rest is just details that justify your insults. But if there is no audience, there is no need for insults, and they'll only discourage your opponent from engaging you any longer, without persuading them. Or your opponent will begin insulting you, and you'll be at an impasse. You

have not won in that situation, and your opponent will likely spread the word about your incapacity to argue.

2) When you're in a situation where the audience will not tolerate explicit insults. This is usually in purely scientific debates, where people want to hear exactly which strings can be pinched together. Whose fingers pinch them is irrelevant. There is of course no such situation ever, anywhere. Who pulls the facts together matters in every debate. But there are situations where the audience still believes the debate should be purely factual, and you must appease the audience. Insults will must stay implicit.

3) When the audience is on your side and your opponent is relentlessly insulting you. This is the fuzziest of the three, because you are often encouraged by the audience to insult right back. In

situations like this, you should judge whether your audience will perceive insulting your opponent as "stooping to their level." If so, the audience will appreciate you sticking to the facts and reasoning, and you'll gain authority for doing so.

In all other cases, slipping in explicit insults will give you an air of authority you wouldn't otherwise have. Think about it: which exhilarates audiences more, two Ivy League students fencing, or two gladiators battling to the death in the Coliseum? Fencing might be fun to watch, simply to see practiced skill and skeletal form at work. But in the Coliseum, the stakes are higher and the lawlessness of it all is downright orgasmic. The audience wants blood to spill. Not spill—*spray*. They are perverse and sadistic. And you must be the embodiment of what the audience wants. Give them their blood in the most creative, fantastic way, a way that challenges their imagination and boggles the mind. They will love you for it.

X X X

Some people believe it is best to embrace the rules of argumentation sanctioned by polite society. They do not win arguments but for pure luck. Etiquette is for the well fed, the unchallenged. Fuck them. Fuck them up. They bleed like everyone else, and embrace the most barbaric aspects of themselves when provoked, showing that they are no better for their rules. The only reason they have lasted so long is by suppressing the poor, the uneducated.

With the rise of literacy, they complain that the unrefined language of the masses is becoming commonplace. It was always commonplace, they just ignored it, in themselves and in the lower classes, which is easy when the lower classes are kept out of classrooms and off pedestals. We're here now, in your classrooms and on your pedestals, and it is high time we destroyed *proper* argument through rhetorical theory the way we destroyed proper grammar through linguistics.

Arguing according to what is effective rather than what is proper is the way of the masses—we've always been more practical like that. There is nothing to be said for doing what is proper at the expense of effectiveness and efficiency. Being proper means following unnecessary rituals, taking pride in nonsense and frivolity. Imagine taking pride in mastering how to hold a teacup with your pinky up. What a joke.

When I look at how we're teaching our children to argue—who, again, are now the children of the masses—what I see taught is how to appeal to the frivolous conventions and rituals of the old academy, the upper classes. This book is full of things you already know, things you already do, but perhaps things you suppressed to appeal to the traditionally literate.

Take pride in your roots, in the industrious ways of the people who, throughout history, haven't had a voice because they couldn't write. Literacy is now yours, so speak up. The upper classes and academics want you to think you still need them. They want you to think they have something to teach you, that you aren't already equipped with tools for effective arguments. If you believe that, you're stupid.

Index

Abraham 138, 143

absurdity 168-9

*The Absurdity of
    Philosophy* 5, 202,
    243

academia 47, 114, 198,
    293, 303

accusations 112, 119,
    158, 200, 262

actor 89-90, 281

ad hominem 295

advantage 72, 100-1,
    104, 106-7, 111-12,
    114, 211, 253, 260-
    1

affair 56-7

agendas 44, 69, 144-5

agreement 13, 82, 93,
    97

Alighieri, Dante 25

allegiances 70, 72

ambiguities 27, 111,
    244, 249-53

apology 22-3, 37-40,
    244

appeal 12, 54-5, 131,
    302

argumentation 2-3, 7,
    16, 91, 99, 136,
    175, 177, 204, 220,
    228, 250, 262, 264,
    300

    limits of 228

arguments 2, 35-6, 40-1,
    76-8, 175-9, 187-8,
    191-6, 206-9, 211-
    13, 217-19, 224-6,
    241-3, 245-57, 259-
    61, 288, 292-3

    many-to-many 77, 80-
    1, 83

    many-to-one 82-3

    one-to-many 77-9

    one-to-one 77-9

Aristotle 146, 285

*Armageddon in
    Retrospect* 173

atheists 17, 71-3

Atlas Shrugged 157

audience 12, 41, 74-80,
    93, 100-1, 110,
    170, 177-8, 218-19,
    221, 225, 279, 282,
    284, 291, 296-300

authority 5, 31, 77, 134-
9, 141-8, 204-10,
212-21, 224-30,
233-4, 236, 242,
251, 278-80, 289,
291-2, 296
centralized 209
delegated 209-10

Bachman, Michelle 119-
20
baseball 52-4
Basic English 46, 48
bee's knees 35, 171-2
*Being Logical: A Guide to
Good Thinking*
263
beliefs 11-13, 69-71, 79,
135, 232, 289
Bin Laden, Osama 285
birthers 119
boundaries 149, 161,
230
Bundy, Ted 29
Bush, George 43, 280-
281, 286

Camus, Albert 4
*Captain Stormfield's Visit
to Heaven* 165,

168-9
Carlin, George 94, 118
charisma 214
chess 244, 268-9
Chomsky, Noam 43
Christianity 25, 249-50
church 25-6, 238
cigarettes 67-8
*Clear Thinking: A
Practical
Introduction* 262
color 59, 183, 185, 239,
241
comedians 31, 94, 98
complaining 35, 50, 103,
220, 301
compliments 126
composure 32, 136, 218
conductor 177-8
consistency 59, 123
context 7, 21, 54, 122,
210, 243-6, 270,
279
contradiction 73, 123-4,
127-9, 131-3, 268
contrastruction 243, 245-
7, 251-2, 255
conversation 1, 9, 14,
97, 100, 103, 110,
283, 288
conviction 126, 234, 249
coping mechanism 92,

94, 96, 154

counterargument 29, 257

coworkers 14, 16, 86, 90, 92

credibility 135-6, 141, 144, 291-2

crime 21, 259

cruelty 215-16

Dawkins, Richard 71, 278-79

death tax 45-6

debaters 41, 243

defeat 206, 209-10

deflecting attacks 219

delineation 176, 194, 196, 199, 202, 274

demands 9-10, 125, 252, 271

democratic process 80

derailment 176-80, 188, 192, 194

Derrida, Jacques 4

Descartes, René 181-4, 276

disagree 48, 73, 134, 139, 165, 243, 246, 279, 297

discrediting 1, 17, 105, 139, 143, 165, 195,

203, 207, 294

dishonesty 3, 13, 61-2, 64-6, 70, 72

The Divine Comedy 25

dominance 216

doublespeak 49

effectiveness 71, 83, 302

ego 75, 157, 218-21, 225, 230-1, 289

embarrassment 86, 98, 125, 243, 269

enemy 29, 43, 47, 85, 205

entertain 98, 196

enthusiasm 69, 121

environment 15, 244

Eschew surplusage. 117, 121-2

estate tax 45-6

etiquette 61, 300

evil 44-5, 50, 68, 145, 157, 160, 223, 281

exceptions 149, 152, 156, 195

exercise 51, 54-5

exhaust, car 67-9

expectations 165, 190, 196

extremes 149, 156-7,

161-2, 195

failure   82-3, 223
family   95, 237
farm towns   190
father   13, 27-8, 44, 181,
   237
fault   35-7, 47, 260
fear   216, 226
feminists   190
films   191
followers   225, 229, 267,
   284
formal debate   1, 41, 93
The Fountainhead   157
Frank, Barney   283
freedom   71, 199-200,
   252
fuel   33, 155

game   35, 53, 192, 245,
   269, 272
genocide   46, 66, 145
goal   1, 17, 22, 38-9, 41-
   3, 73, 78, 80, 89-
   90, 135, 222, 253,
   294
God   17, 21, 71, 268
Gorgias   200
government   45, 49, 136,

234, 236
grammar   77, 79, 113,
   301
group   12-13, 57, 67-8,
   80-1, 83, 92
grumfel   183-5
guilty   35-6, 38, 66, 196,
   262

hasty   282, 284
hate   168, 170, 226
hedonism   158
history   7, 113, 118, 143,
   158-9, 179, 295,
   303
Hitler, Adolf   46, 145,
   152, 280-1, 283
Hollywood   190, 196
Holocaust   66
honesty   61, 223, 226
human sacrifices   138-9,
   143
humans   75, 123, 158-9,
   161, 223
hypocrisies   67-70, 72-3,
   81, 114, 188, 195,
   260

I think, therefore I am.
   179-86

identity 77, 274, 277-83,
      289, 292-3, 295
ideologies 66, 69, 73,
      146, 148-50, 152,
      156, 194, 222, 235
immorality 232, 234
immutability 240, 242
implications 27, 187,
      270, 282, 284
individuals 12, 82-3, 238
inflections 89, 109, 111-
      12
information 7-8, 44, 64,
      89, 101, 134, 136-
      8, 141, 146, 266,
      276
insincerity 37, 39
instructions 5, 7-8, 10,
      15, 19, 22, 24, 26,
      28, 33-4, 37, 175,
      258, 275-6
insults 36, 82, 216, 291-
      3, 295-9
   explicit 288, 297-8
   implicit 288, 297
intelligent design 210
intentional 164, 170, 256
Internet 62, 79, 82
issue 20, 38, 41, 119,
      123, 199-200
   moral 233

Jesus 224
Jews 138-40, 143
joke books 85-6, 98
jokes 14, 16, 31, 85-7,
      92, 94, 96-7, 106,
      164, 195, 202, 302
judgments 223, 229, 234

killing 27, 93
kindness 225
King, Larry 119-20

language 1-2, 7-10, 12-
      13, 15, 48-51, 54,
      100, 107, 113, 133-
      4, 175, 179, 186,
      199, 202, 258
   body 100, 108, 112
   English 46, 117
   ordinary 25, 132, 179-
      80, 186, 198, 301
   philosophical 180
   spoken 76, 100, 114
laughter 16-17, 92-9,
      167
law of attraction 150-1,
      153-6
law of identity 274, 276-
      7, 285

270

law of non-contradiction 268, 285
laws of physics 241, 268
laziness 126, 231
leech 215
legal system 50, 80, 268
listening 29, 32, 70, 78, 88-9, 101, 108, 110-11, 129, 135, 193
literacy 114, 301-3
logic 147, 223, 265-74, 277, 285, 287
  badge 265, 272
love 63, 88, 90, 126, 169-70, 188-90, 195-6, 300
luck 211, 213, 231, 300
Luntz, Frank 43, 48-50, 61-2, 64-5, 70

Machiavelli, Niccolò 3-4, 204, 232, 236
manufactured knowledge 71
Marx, Karl 224
masses 11, 47, 301-2
McInerny, D. Q. 263
mediums 100, 106-7
Mein Kampf 46
metaphor 170, 294

minor victories 208
mischaracterization 256
morality 156, 160, 188, 234
mother 235, 256-7
movie 62, 186-90, 193, 195-7, 200
murder 27, 30, 93

Nazis 50, 152, 281
negation 270-1, 280
neighbors 103
nemesis 43, 50
neoconservatives 43-5, 50
The New Rhetoric 263
Newspeak 48-9
Nietzsche, Friedrich 4
Nineteen Eighty-Four 48-9
non-contradiction 268, 285
nonsense 96, 265, 302
nuance 50, 270-1

Obama, Barack 119, 144-5, 283
objectivists 157, 162
off-track 33, 97, 113-14, 177, 179

Ogden, C. K. 46
onlookers 66, 80, 104, 131
opponent 17, 93, 104-6, 124-5, 127, 131-4, 139, 141-4, 170, 176-7, 210, 224-5, 252-5, 288, 290-2, 297-9
oppression 234, 236
organization 4-5, 8, 80-1, 128, 140, 145, 148, 152, 203, 205, 237, 245, 253, 277, 281
Orwell, George 46, 48-9
Orwellian 49

pain 35-6, 65, 164, 201, 295
paint 170, 239, 241
party 25, 115-16, 166
passion 69, 126, 138, 198
pawns 275-6
people's attention 44, 108
Perelman, Chaim 4, 70, 263
perfecting style 98
persuasions 41, 156,

216, 218
philosophy 2, 5, 67, 146-7, 157, 179, 186, 191, 194, 198, 202, 243
phrase 7, 44, 121, 170, 179-80, 289
physicists 51
physics 51, 177, 241, 268
Plato 146
plumber 274, 276-7
politics 3, 119, 142, 204, 234
pornography 190-1
postmodernists 67, 72
practiced talent 213, 299
praise 82, 208
presentations 85, 87, 90, 224
presidential candidate 14-15
Presley, Elvis 278-281, 284
presumptions, failed 269
pride 213, 302-3
The Prince 204
propaganda 46, 48, 69
punctuation 121-2
puppy-dog eyes 15-16
Pythagoras 284-5

Rand, Ayn   27, 52, 141-
        2, 157-8, 160-2,
        190-1, 207, 241,
        269, 278, 281-2,
        285
rationalism   147, 158
reactions   29-30, 32, 110
rebuttals   106, 198, 206
relationship   249, 289
religious leaders   235
representatives, elected
        45
responsibility   94, 131,
        138
revolt   142, 207, 226
rhetoric   3-4, 10, 13-16,
        35, 40, 91, 120,
        175, 200, 216, 287
    argumentative   17
    effective   14, 16
    ineffective   14
    non-argumentative   17
rhetorical authority   4, 7-
        8, 13, 15, 204, 211,
        215, 217-18, 232,
        241
rhetorical tactics   15, 17,
        103, 266
rhetorical theory   263,
        301
risk   142, 279-80, 282

roommate   19, 22, 26,
        239
Ruchlis, Hy   262
rules   56, 60, 65, 117,
        122, 156, 175, 220,
        222, 225, 268-9,
        276, 300-1
Ruth, Babe   53

sacrifice   118, 223, 253
sarcasm   39, 164-5, 168,
        170
scenario   39, 93, 181
The Secret   149-52, 156
self-help   86-7, 149, 157
self-interest   157-9
semantic choice   26, 30,
        33-4, 49, 145, 241,
        246
sentences   10-11, 27, 30,
        32, 88, 107-8, 115,
        121, 133, 180, 192,
        268, 271, 275, 277
sex   60, 191
shame   211, 248
simplification   243
sincere   39
skepticism   217
slavery   172, 222
smoking bans   69
snozzits   183, 185

social norms   61, 76

socialist movements   237

society   61, 189-90, 195-6, 238, 281, 300

Socrates   146, 200

sophistry   146-7

sources   4, 136, 210

speaker   23, 79, 244

speech   85, 90, 100-2, 104, 106, 109, 111-12, 118, 170, 172, 174

standards   3, 61, 69, 160

statistics   68, 101

status quo   12, 74, 78

story   52, 54, 88, 96, 165, 173, 187-8

Strauss, Leo   44

strawman   255-62

strength   211, 252

strings   293-4, 298

stutters   103, 112-13, 121

submission   201, 206-7, 216, 231

support   41, 50, 58, 80, 143, 205, 214-15, 217

surrealism   164, 168-70

surreality   164, 168-9

syllables   117-19, 121-2

symbol   189, 195

sympathy   35

tactics   1, 41, 50, 64, 104, 120, 146, 175, 213, 222

tangents   71, 97, 121, 164

taxes   45, 55, 136

terrorist attacks   285

theists   72-3

traditions   78, 146

  argumentative   211

train   177-9, 194

transitive verb   180, 182

trust   10, 58, 79, 141, 216-18, 221, 226-8

truth   2, 5, 10-14, 47, 56, 62, 67, 156, 216, 226, 234, 263, 266, 268

  effectual   222

  popular   11

truthfulness   13, 223

attack   57-8, 105, 142, 212, 250, 255, 289

Twain, Mark   117-18, 122, 165

Ulysses   101

United States   43, 119

writing   100-1, 107-10,
            112, 114-15, 118,
            122, 186

violence   244

vocabulary   21, 24, 37,
            43, 46, 48, 51, 54-
            5, 125, 175, 262,
            289

voice   15, 37, 82, 109,
            111, 121, 136

Vonnegut, Kurt   172-4

weak spot   70, 212

whims   7-8, 109, 241,
            287

whores, corporate   43,
            115

wife   5, 19, 56-7, 60, 63,
            126, 172, 239, 255

winning   38, 41-2, 60, 93,
            134, 148, 175, 206-
            7, 214, 221-2, 244,
            262, 295

Wittgenstein, Ludwig   4

women   162, 191, 240,
            283

words   7-9, 15, 21-2, 30-
            4, 44, 54-5, 62, 65,
            88-90, 108, 112-22,
            161, 184-6, 200-1,
            244-5, 290-2

World Wars   46, 235